Okyere Bonna, MBA

Vocabulary Practice for Grades 6 & 7

Copyright © 2012 by **Okyere Bonna**
Library of Congress Control Number: **2012908191**
Soft cover: ISBN 978-1-61957-056-6
E-book: ISBN 978-1-61957-057-3

AMAZON EDITION
ISBN-13: 978-1475201963
ISBN-10: 1475201966

This book was printed in the United States of America.
Okab
P.O. Box 79029
Charlotte, NC 28271
To order additional copies of this book, contact:
www.Amazon.com
Or
https://tsw.createspace.com/title/3851895

Email: okab.publishing@gmail.com

Vocabulary Practice for Grades 6 & 7

Okyere Bonna MBA, MSEd

**Dedicated to my 7th grade daughter,
Petra-Maria**

Table of contents

Introduction

This work book was first designed for my daughter, who was in 7th grade AIG program to help her prepare for the Independent School Entrance Exam (ISEE). My daughter, who was in the Academically Gifted Class (AIG) in one the best Public schools in the state, was transitioning into a private school. Barely a week before the exam I was surprised to find out that my daughter had not been able to master the Sample Test Questions I bought for her. In quizzing her about the meanings of the answer choices she had made, I found her very deficient. I was shocked because my daughter is an avid reader. She told me these are not the words she finds in the course of her readings. She told me, "Daddy I don't have any material to study for the vocabulary section of the English test." My immediate reaction was to ask her to use the dictionary. Then I realize that could not be very helpful. So looking at the sample questions I decided to create some worksheets for her to help her practice for the exams.

This workbook is designed for the 6th and 7th grader to help you become familiar with some basic vocabulary words for your standardized test. I recommended that you **read through (or study) the glossary section first before you start working on the worksheets**. After going through these worksheets you will have a broad idea of what to expect on your test day and feel comfortable.

UNIT 1

GLOSSARY

&

Vocabulary Words

Word List A

abruptness	disgust	homely	realistic
admire	disorderly	honest	reluctance
affection	disputed	illegally	sharp
agile	distasteful	indifference	solitary
alone	doubtful	insight	soothe
anxious	eagerness	keen	suddenness
boredom	ease	nicely	understanding
claimed	elegant	nimble	unruly
clearly	extent	pacify	unwillingness
dejection	fatigue	panic	weakly
disagreement	feared	playful	weariness
disbelieving	feebly	praise	
discovered	forgive	proved	

Word List B

adapt	dense	greedy	ravine
analyze	departure	haughty	repeal
announcement	detrimental	incident	replenish
anticipate	drenched	indicate	responsive
barren	elevated	insolent	revere
blunt	endanger	intricate	sentimental
celebrate	endeavor	lofty	similar
complex	episode	omit	suppose
concise	excite	optimistic	suspicious
conclusion	exemplify	pinnacle	thrive
conform	extreme	plume	torrid
construct	fertile	postponed	
core	formal	presume	

Word List C

acknowledge	endanger	noncommittal	resume
anticipate	exemplify	obstinate	retire
aspiration	falter	peak	subside
cautious	flourish	permission	supplement
certify	fragile	persevere	thriving
characteristic	gullible	prone	thwarted
controversial	intended	protective	verbal
disappoint	inundated	quantitative	
dissect	migrate	refusal	
economize	negative	reject	

Word List D

abhor	deliberate	govern	occupations
ambidextrous	detest	grievances	petty
arbitrary	drastic	hazards	pretend
assent	elegant	hectic	react
bashful	entrust	intentional	rustic
commodities	extravagant	legitimate	sinister
conceal	extreme	logical	
defensive	flamboyant	mystify	

A: Definitions

Abruptness (uhbruhptnuhs)
The quality of happening with headlong haste or without warning. Sudden
> The music stopped abruptly

Admire (admiir) *verb*
1. To look up to someone or something with respect
2. Look up to with appreciation.
Synonyms: appreciate, honor, consider, esteem, respect, cherish, regard
Antonyms: disdain, scorn, abhor

> I admire the talent of that piano player.
> I admire my grandmother a great deal.
> During fall, I like to walk through the park and admire the colorful leaves.

Affection (uhfEHkshuhn) *noun*
1. A positive feeling of liking.
2. A feeling of kindness, fondness, love for someone or something
Synonyms: feeling, tenderness, emotion, devotion, love, warmth, attachment, fondness
Antonyms: antipathy, coldness, disaffection, insensibility, repugnance, indifference

> Dogs react to kindness by showing affection.
> Calvary Medical Clinic staff have a lot of affection for their patients.
> Hugging is one way to show affection.

Agile (ajuhl) *adjective*
1. Mentally quick.
2. Characterized by quickness, lightness, and ease of movement; nimble. Mentally quick or alert: an agile mind.
Synonyms: nimble, limber, spry, dexterous
Antonyms: awkward, clumsy, heavy, torpid, slow, inert

> The agile athletes floated gracefully across the court.
> The athlete is agile and quick.

Alone (uhlohn) *adjective, adverb*
1. To be by yourself.
2. When you are by your self
3. Without other persons or things.
Synonyms: isolated, secluded, detached, lone, solo, removed, unaccompanied, only, lonesome,
             unaided, unattended, solitary
Antonyms: accompanied, attended, together, jointly

> It is not safe to go into the jungle alone.
> Living alone in the palace has made the old queen eccentric.
> The hermit lives alone up in the hills.

Anxious (aNGkshuhs) *adjective*
1. A feeling of uneasiness. To feel worried, nervous, or eager. You may feel this before a big math test.
2. Afraid or nervous about what may happen
Synonyms: thirsty, apprehensive, ardent, aghast, uneasy, nervous, eager, fearful, worried, impatient

Antonyms: confident, relieved, ease, inert, hesitant, careless, reluctant

Cameron is anxious for his sister to have a baby so he can be an uncle.
Everyone was anxious to fight and get the war over.
Today they're anxious to play, their competitive juices are flowing.

Boredom   (bawrduhm) *noun*
1. The feeling of having nothing to do, a tedious state
2. The state of feeling tired, restless, and uninterested
   Boredom makes some people feel sleepy.
   Nana Afua yawned repeatedly due to her boredom in social studies class.
   Patrick started to play in his desk because of boredom.

Claimed   (klaymd)
1. To say that something belongs to you
2. To demand as yours or to state something strongly.
   She claimed her undying love of Collie dogs.
   They claimed they did not despoil the store, but they were caught on video camera.
   The Phantom of the Opera was an imposter and not really the Angel of Music as he claimed to be.

Clearly   (klihrlee) *adverb*
Clean and free from anything that makes it hard to see.
   I didn't hear clearly so I asked him to repeat the sentence.

Dejection   *noun*
1. A state of melancholy depression.
2. Lowness of spirits; sadness; depression
   The friends of the deceased man felt very melancholy and dejected.

Disagreement   (dihsuhgreemuhnt) *noun*
1. Lack of understanding or unity
2. A quarrel; not able to come to an agreement; not of the same opinion
Synonyms: dissension, opposition, fight, dispute, conflict, quarrel, feud
 Antonym: accord

   We can reconcile this disagreement with just a little compromise.
   It will do no good to wrestle over this disagreement.
   Our chess game ended in a disagreement.

Disbelieving   (dihsbuhleevihNG)
Reject as false; refuse to accept.
   His excuse for not doing his homework was disbelieving to his teacher.

Discovered   (dihskuhvurd) *adjective, verb*
1. Find unexpectedly.
2. See for the first time; make a discovery.
3. To find, see, or learn something, usually for the first time
   The claim that Christopher Columbus discovered America is questionable as the Indians were already on the land.
   I discovered that ants are very smart little bugs.
   The police discovered a weapon hidden in the house.

Disgust (dihsguhst) *noun, verb*
1. Strong feelings of dislike.
2. A feeling of horrified distaste for something
Synonyms: nausea, appall, queasiness, distaste
Antonyms: please, delight, partiality, desire, liking

> My mother looked at my messy bedroom and gave a groan of disgust.
> Her impropriety caused the audience to boo in disgust.
> The student's reactions to the film ran the gamut from exhilaration to disgust.

Disorderly (dihsawrdurlee) *adjective*
 Not in order, not disciplined
Synonyms: untidy, messy, disorganized, cluttered
Antonyms: neat, tidy

> Why is this place so disorderly?
> I am not disorderly, I am methodical.

Disputed (dihspyootuhd) *adjective, verb*
1. Open to debate.
2. Argued; disagreed; fought over
3. To argue; to quarrel.
> Bill and Joe disputed who won the video game.
> She disputed her claim to royalty.

Distasteful (dihstaystfuhl) *adjective*
1. Not pleasing in odor or taste.
2. Unpleasant, disagreeable, objectionable or offensive
Antonyms: pleasant, appealing

> That remark was crude and distasteful!
> The audience found the speaker's crude joke quite distasteful.

Doubtful (doutfuhl) *adjective*
1. Open to suspicion.
2. To be unsure about something.
Synonyms: unlikely, dubious, uncertain, impossible, questionable, improbable
Antonyms: certain, sure, indubitable

> I am doubtful about what he said.
> If it rains it is doubtful we will be able to go to the park.
> I am doubtful we will have practice today since it is raining.

Eagerness (eegurnuhs)
1. A positive feeling of wanting to push ahead with something.
2. A strong desire to do something.
> Katherine has played well in recent weeks, and her eagerness was evident at her piano recital.

Ease (eez) *noun, verb*
1. Move gently or carefully.
2. Freedom from constraint or embarrassment.
3. Make easier.
4. To make less worried, pained or troubled.

Synonyms: rest, comfort, prosperity, abundance, calm, relaxation, soothe, leisure, repose
Antonyms: toil, awkwardness, aggravate, worsen, effort

> Jamie had to ease her sister's fear of the dark.
> He adapted to his new surroundings with minimal ease.
> Taking aspirin helped ease his headache.

Elegant (EHluhguhnt) *adjective*
1. Of seemingly effortless beauty in form or proportion.
2. Something beautiful, suggesting great wealth.
3. Refined or tastefully lavish, excellent, splendid.
Synonyms: fancy, exquisite, fine, graceful, stylish, tasteful, refined
Antonyms: coarse, crude, plain, inelegant, deformed, unsymmetrical

> My mother's elegant pose made a beautiful picture.
> She looked like an elegant princess in her new dress.
> The ship's furnishings and food were sumptuous and elegant.

Extent (ihkstEHnt) *noun*
The range, distance, or space over or through which something extends.
Synonyms: magnitude, range, sweep, matter
Antonyms: diminution, restriction, limitation

Fatigue (fuhteeg) *noun, verb*
1. Great tiredness resulting from hard physical or mental work.
2. A tired felling that lowers your level of activity.
Synonyms: tiredness, weakness, exhaustion, weariness
Antonyms: energy, vigor, energize, refresh

> Doing the same thing over and over is tedious, causing mental fatigue.
> Doing the same thing over and over is boring, causing mental fatigue.
> He was hospitalized for extreme fatigue.

Feared (fihrd)
Be uneasy or apprehensive about.
> The soldiers feared a raid.
> The woman feared the elevator because of her claustrophobia.
> When Alex brought home his report card, he greatly feared his parent's discipline.

Feebly (feeblee) *adjective, adverb*   Not having strength or sick; weak
> Weak and tired, the man walked feebly to a bench to rest.
> Feebly the old man walked to the store for food.

Forgive (furgihv) *verb*
1. To stop blaming or feeling anger toward someone; pardon or excuse.
2. Stop blaming somebody or stop feeling angry with somebody about something.
Synonyms: acquit, clear, absolve, excuse, condone, pardon
Antonyms: blame, condemn

> To err is human, to forgive divine.
> When you don't forgive someone, you feel bad.

Homely (hohmlee) *adjective*
1. Not attractive in appearance; plain.
2. Unattractive, plain, simple, ordinary.
3. Not good-looking. Plain and simple.
Synonyms: unostentatious, unhandsome, plain, unlovely, unpretty, unattractive, unbeautiful, simple, ugly
Antonyms: sophisticated, comely, beautiful, refined, handsome

    Sarah was a very homely person.
    Abraham Lincoln was often described as a homely man in many ways.
    The homely little girl could not get a date for the prom.

Honest (onuhst) *adjective*
1. Capable of being trusted, not stealing, cheating, or lying.
2. True to yourself and others.
Synonyms: trustworthy, upright, honorable, genuine, unfeigned, just, good, conscientious, truthful
Antonyms: dishonest, deceitful, dishonorable, vicious, improper

    Devious people can never have true success, until they learn to be honest.
    Please give your honest and open opinion on the questionnaire.
    If you are an honest person people will trust you.

Illegally (ihleeguhlee) *adjective, adverb*
Not acceptable, lawful or within the law
    If you park illegally, the police will impound your car.
    He illegally impersonated a police officer.

Indifference (ihndihfuruhns) *noun*
1. Apathy demonstrated by an absence of emotional reactions.
2. The trait of remaining calm and seeming not to care; a casual lack of concern.
3. A don't care attitude.
Synonyms: inattention, unconcern, apathy
Antonyms: importance, significance, gravity, eagerness, weight

    Adu showed indifference when it came to watching boxing.
    It is not good for a driver to show a blithe indifference for the safety of others on the highway.
    The student's indifference to school will soon come back to haunt him.

Insight (ihnsiit) *noun*
1. Clear or deep perception of a situation.
2. The power or act of seeing into a situation.
3. The ability to perceive the true nature of something.
    John seemed almost like a prophet with his insight.
    His insight into the problems made him the first choice for chairman.

Keen *noun, verb, adjective*
1. Having or demonstrating ability to recognize or draw fine distinctions.
2. Intense or sharp.
3. Sharp and quick with the five senses; eager
Synonyms: sensitive, sharp, ardent, eager, acute, avid, fine, perceptive
Antonyms: indifferent, dull, blunt, reluctant, apathetic

    Hawks have keen sight,

He has a very keen sense of humor.

Nicely (niislee)   Good, pleasant, agreeable, pretty, kind, polite, etc.,

Nimble (nihmbuhl) *adjective*
1. Moving quickly and lightly.
2. Mentally quick.
3. The opposite of awkward; graceful
4. Quick in thinking and understanding.
Synonyms: brisk, adroit, handy, lively, agile, active, deft, quick, spry, sprightly, clever

The old woman was still able to do needlework because she had nimble fingers.
My little brother's favorite nursery rhyme is "Jack Be Nimble."
All athletes must be nimble in order to compete.

Pacify (pasuhfii) *verb*
1. Cause to be more favorably inclined; gain the good will of.
2. To make peaceful or calm; to soothe
Antonyms: agitate, alarm, anger, aggravate, excite, exasperate, irritate

We tried to pacify the baby's crying but only her mother could calm her down.
The mother reached for a toy to pacify the crying baby.

Panic (panihk) *noun, verb*
1. An overwhelming feeling of fear and anxiety.
2. Unreasonable fear causing someone to lose control
3. Excited, scared, don't know what to do.
Synonyms: scream, fear, howl, fright, terror, alarm, distress, horror, riot, dread, dismay

Stay calm, and don't panic!
It is sensible not to panic in the face of a dilemma.
If you feel you are in danger, do not panic.

Playful (playfuhl) *adjective*
Full of play; fond of playing
Synonyms: frolicsome, joking, lively, frisky, amusing, energetic
Antonyms: serious, solemn, somber, dull

The puppy was very playful.
Joshua was in a very playful mood.

Praise (prayz) *noun, verb*
1. To honor with words or song.
2. To say something good about something
Synonyms: hail, compliments, approve, applaud, extol, approval, admire, commend, acclaim, bless,
         compliment, recommend, recognition, commendation
Antonyms: blame, censure, disapproval, disapprove, discommend, criticize, criticism

Everyone likes to get praise.
The conductor had high praise for the guest soloist's performance.
Sometimes faint praise is worse than no praise at all.

Proved (proovd)
1. Established beyond doubt.
2. To show that something is true or correct.

> Her intellectual prowess was proved by the test results.
> His scowl proved he was angry.
> He proved to be an insidious enemy.

Realistic (reeuhlihstihk) *adjective*
1. Having or showing an inclination to face facts and deal with them sensibly
2. Being real; common sense decisions
3. Using facts and good sense to evaluate people, things, or situations; concerned with the practical; resembling real life
Antonyms: unrealistic, fanciful

> The painting is very realistic.
> Realistic stories are often about family life and friends.

Reluctance (rihluhktuhns) *noun*
1. The state of not wanting to do something.
2. Lack of enthusiasm: unwillingness or lack of enthusiasm

> Her reluctance to read aloud was due to her shyness.
> His reluctance to get on the plane was due to his fear of heights.

Sharp (shorp) *noun, adjective, adverb*
1. A thin, fine edge or a pointed tip.
2. Having a thin cutting edge or fine point.
Synonyms: abrupt, cutting, alert, keen, keep, pointed, acute
Antonyms: dull, blunt, slow, thick, obtuse, knobbed, gradual

> Hawks have sharp talons.

Solitary (soluhtEHree) *adjective*
1. Lacking companions or companionship.
2. Without the company of others. Single, lone. Far away from society.
Synonyms: single, isolated, lone
Antonyms: accompanied, social, gregarious, busy, popular

> Earlier he spent 12 years in prison, much of it in solitary confinement.
> Sometimes I take refuge in the library where it is quiet and solitary.
> Many victims of the Holocaust were kept in solitary confinement.

Soothe (sooth) *verb*
1. Give moral or emotional strength to.
2. To please by praise or attention.
3. Truly or really; in agreement with the truth, facts, or reality.
4. To quiet or calm someone
Synonyms: relieve, relax, settle, quiet, ease, calm
Antonyms: irritate, upset, aggravate, excite, exacerbate

> The medicine will soothe the burning skin.
> The medicine will soothe the pain of the cut.
> She gently talked to the injured pup trying to soothe its fear.

Suddenness (suhduhnnuhs)   The quality of happening with headlong haste or without warning.

Understanding (uhndurstandihNG) *noun, adjective*
1. Knowing what something means or how it works
2. Appreciating the reasons for a mistake.
Synonyms: appreciation, agreement, compromise, deal, bargain, concept, grasp, arrangement,
            comprehension
Antonyms: insensitive, unsympathetic, misunderstand, ignorance

His poor diction kept me from understanding a word he said.
An understanding of human anatomy is important to a dancer.
Cognition means learning and understanding something.

Unruly (uhnroolee) *adjective*
1. Unwilling to submit to authority.
2. Not following rules; hard to manage
3. Impossible to discipline; refusing to obey
Synonyms: boisterous, intractable, disobedient, uncontrollable, disorderly, rowdy, wild, turbulent,
            raucous, unmanageable
Antonyms: docile, obedient, tractable

The unruly children were not allowed recess time.
An unruly class is a teacher's worst nightmare.
He was punished for his unruly behaviour.

Unwillingness (uhnwihlihNGnihs)
Not wanting to do something
Akua's bad temper and unwillingness to compromise caused him to be alienated from his peers.

Weakly (weeklee)   Lacking physical strength or vitality.
She became very weakly when she was sick.

Weariness (wihreenuhs)
1. To be exhausted - very tired
2. Worn out in strength, energy, or freshness
A feeling of weariness came over us at the end of the mile run in P.E. class.
After playing in the soccer tournament the team collapsed due to weariness.

B: Definitions

Adapt (uhdapt) *verb*
1. Changing to get used to something new.
2. To adjust to a new situation or surrounding.
<u>Synonyms:</u> change, fit, conform
<u>Antonyms:</u> unfit, misfit, misapply

I must adapt to my new school.
I know you will adapt to your new surrounding quickly.

Analyze (anuhliiz) *verb*
1. Figuring out something by looking at its parts.
2. To study carefully in order to determine what something is, what its parts are, or how its parts fit together.
<u>Synonyms:</u> evaluate, study, examine, investigate
<u>Antonyms:</u> compose, compound, construct

It is not always easy to analyze what went wrong.

Announcement (uhnounsmuhnt) *noun*
A formal printed notice, as of a wedding or other event
The announcement was greeted with happiness.

Anticipate (antihsuhpayt) *verb*
1. Regard something as probable or likely.
2. Act in advance of; deal with ahead of time.
3. Realize beforehand.
4. Make a prediction about; tell in advance.
5. Be excited or anxious about.
6. To foresee, to realize beforehand
<u>Synonyms:</u> expect, foresee, prevent, forestall, predict, see, await, divine
<u>Antonyms:</u> remember, recollect, remedy, recall

Do you anticipate what time the meeting will end?

Barren (baruhn) *noun, adjective*
Not able to produce growing plants or crops.
<u>Synonyms:</u> infertile, desolate, sterile, unproductive, bare, empty, effete, unfertile
<u>Antonyms:</u> fertile, lush, productive, fecund

The doctor told my aunt that she was barren.

Blunt (bluhnt) *verb, adjective*
1. Used of a knife or other blade; not sharp.
2. Make less sharp.
3. Abrupt; frank; outspoken.
<u>Synonyms:</u> obtuse, tactless, dull, brusque, unsharpened, short, direct, frank, candid
<u>Antonyms:</u> tactful, subtle, sharp, keen

The knife was too blunt to cut a tomato!
My uncle gave me some blunt advice.

Celebrate (sEHluhbrayt) *verb*
1. A day or holiday when people do something enjoyable.
2. To have parties or fun to enjoy a special day.
3. To do something special or have festivities to observe an event or day.
4. To do certain things because of a special occasion.
Synonyms: honor, observe, keep, commemorate

Memorial Day is an annual holiday that we celebrate in May.

Complex (komplEHks) *noun, adjective*
Intricate, not simple, composed of two or more related parts
Synonyms: composite, complicated, compound, knotty, hard, involved, difficult, intricate,
          sophisticated, elaborate
Antonyms: simple, easy

That is a complex math problem.

Concise (kuhnsiis) *adjective*
1. Say a lot with few words.
2. Expressed in a few words.
Synonyms: short, succinct, brief, condensed
Antonyms: verbose, wordy, long, redundant

Be concise when you are writing your report.

Conclusion (kuhnkloozhuhn) *noun*
The end of a book, play, or movie.
Synonyms: finish, close, judgment, finale, cessation, termination, cease, stop, end, deduction, inference
Antonyms: beginning, start, inauguration

The author will astound her readers with the conclusion of the book.

Conform (kuhnfawrm) *verb*
1. Adapt or conform oneself to new or different conditions.
2. To follow an established pattern or standard
3. To behave or think like others
Synonyms: follow, harmonize, observe, adjust, comply with, suit, obey, agree
Antonyms: differ, disagree, diverge

The new student tried to conform to the rules of the new school.

Construct (kuhnstruhkt) *noun, verb*
To build something or create.
Synonyms: manufacture, produce, build, assemble, form, fabricate, frame, establish, raise, make

Scientists use fossil records to construct a geologic time scale.

Core (kawr) *noun, verb*

1. This deepest layer is at the center of Earth.
2. the innermost layer of Earth
3. the innermost layer of Earth.
4. the hard center of an apple or pear
<u>Synonyms:</u> purport, midst, kernel, center, staple, seed, nut, essence, middle

> The mantle of the earth is next to the core.
> The center of the earth is called the core.
> The core of the Sun is made up of helium.

Dense (dEHns) *adjective*
1. Closely crowded together.
2. Hard to pass through because of dense growth.
3. very thick or crowded in space
<u>Synonyms:</u> dull, compact, stupid, close, thick, solid, dumb, tight
<u>Antonyms:</u> bright, quick, subtle, thin, rare, intelligent, clever

> The smog in Louisville is very dense.

Departure (dihporchur) *noun*
To leave, especially to go on a journey.
<u>Synonyms:</u> aberration, leaving, withdrawal, divergence, exodus, going, exit
<u>Antonyms:</u> arrival, conformity

> Everyone was sadden by her departure.
> Please affirm the departure time.

Detrimental (dEHtruhmEHntuhl) *adjective*
1. When something is very damaging to something else
2. Anything that causes damage or injury.
<u>Synonyms:</u> unfavorable, adverse, injurious, negative, ill
<u>Antonyms:</u> beneficial, profitable, augmentative

> Using drugs is detrimental to your health.

Drenched (drEHncht) *adjective, verb*   Soaked or very wet .
> The rain drenched the people waiting for the bus.
> Billy stood at the door drenched by the rain.

Elevated (EHluhvaytihd)   Raised to a higher level.
> She has been elevated to manager.

Endanger (EHndaynjur) *verb*
To put in a dangerous situation; to threaten.
<u>Antonyms:</u> cover, defend, protect, shield

> The pollution will endanger the crops.

Endeavor (ihndEHvur) *noun, verb*
1. A purposeful or industrious undertaking (especially one that requires effort or boldness).
2. Try hard; Make an effort; strive.

Synonyms: try, undertake, attempt, seek, strive

I only ask that you always endeavor to do your best.

Episode (EHpuhsohd) *noun*
1. A happening that is distinctive in a series of related events.
2. A brief section of a literary or dramatic work that forms part of a connected series.
3. A part of a broadcast serial.
4. An occurrence that has happened during the course of a day.
Synonyms: development, event, incident, occurrence

The last episode of the story made me cry.

Excite (ihksiit) *verb*
 A sudden decline in strength or number or importance.
Synonyms: move, provoke, stimulate, agitate, rouse, interest, inspire, stir, prime, arouse, thrill
Antonyms: calm, appease, allay, deaden, quiet

Do not excite the dog because he might bite you.

Exemplify (ihgzEHmpluhfii) *verb*   To illustrate or to serve as an example or by example.
Soldier's fighting in Iraq exemplify mettlesome behavior.

Extreme (ihkstreem) *noun, adjective*
1. One of two ends or opposites
2. Existing in the greatest possible degree.
Synonyms: fanatic, intense, unusual, utmost, uttermost, immoderate, great, tremendous
Antonyms: initial, primal, moderate, judicious

He was in extreme pain.
People in the desert live in extreme heat.

Fertile (furtuhl) *adjective*
1. Marked by great fruitfulness.
2. Bearing in abundance especially offspring.
3. Able to produce more, especially land that is full of nutrients.
4. Rich soil that is good for growing crops.
Synonyms: productive, rich, fruitful, bountiful
Antonyms: sterile, barren, feeble, ineffective, inactive, poor, infertile

The flowers will thrive in the fertile soil.

Formal (fawrmuhl) *adjective*
1. Proper and not casual.
2. Very correct, following all the rules of conduct and/or dress
3. Done in a proper way. A formal letter or statement is stiff, rigid, proper, and perfect.
Synonyms: stately, conventional, ceremonious, proper, solemn, regular, nominal, official
Antonyms: informal, irregular, unconventional, incomplete, inadequate

He made a formal statement about running for mayor.
The formal name for your collarbone is the clavicle.
David rented a tuxedo to wear to the formal dance.

Greedy (greedee) *adjective*
 Wanting to have more than you need
Synonyms: jealous, possessive, acquisitive, covetous, grasping, avaricious, selfish
Antonyms: abstemious, abstinent, indifferent

>   Don't be greedy and eat all the cookies.

Haughty (hawtee) *adjective*
 Arrogant; vainly proud; showing disdain to those one views as unworthy.
Synonyms: proud, conceited, vain, arrogant
Antonyms: humble, modest, lowly

>   Her haughty attitude did not make her a very popular girl.

Incident (ihnsuhduhnt) *noun, adjective*
1. A single distinct event.
2. An event that is unusual.
Synonyms: happening, experience, event, affair

>   The sad incident was still very vivid in his memory.

Indicate (ihnduhkayt) *verb*
 To show; to make known.
Synonyms: point out, suggest, testify, hint, imply, mark, show, argue, reveal, designate
Antonyms: conceal, contradict

>   Please indicate on the map where we are.

Insolent (ihnsuhluhnt) *adjective*
1. Showing lack of respect to rank or authority.
2. Rude or arrogant in conduct and speech
Synonyms: impudent, supercilious, audacious, overbearing
Antonyms: deferential, respectful, polite, courteous, meek

>   Nick's remarks were insolent.
>   The boy behaved like an insolent child.

Intricate (ihntruhkuht) *adjective*
1. Containing many details or small parts that are skillfully made or assembled
2. Complicated or tangled, highly involved.
Synonyms: elaborate, sophisticated, involved, complex, complicated, fancy, knotty, detailed
Antonyms: simple, plain, uninvolved

>   We could see many details in the intricate painting.

Lofty (lawftee) *adjective*
1. Of imposing height; especially standing out above others.
2. Having or displaying great dignity or nobility.
3. Very high or very high moral value.
Synonyms: towering, insolent, high, grand, tall, utopian, overbearing
Antonyms: low, short, depressed

>   The Pharisees had a lofty attitude towards other people.

The teacher has lofty goals for her students.

Omit (ohmiht) *verb*
1. Prevent from being included or considered or accepted.
2. Leave undone or leave out.
3. To leave undone or leave out.
4. To leave out or unmentioned.
Synonyms: neglect, exclude, forget
Antonyms: add, include

When you do your homework, omit questions 11, 15 and 19.
I must remember to omit my error on the final draft.

Optimistic (optuhmihstihk) *adjective*
Hopeful that things will turn out in the best possible way.
Synonyms: trusting, hopeful, confident, positive
Antonyms: pessimistic, gloomy

She is optimistic about her success in school.
I am optimistic that summer vacation will be here soon!

Pinnacle (pihnuhkuhl) *noun, verb*
1. A lofty peak.
2. (Architecture) a slender upright spire at the top of a buttress of tower.
3. The highest point; a spire
Antonyms: nadir, bottom

The pinnacle of the tower was in need of repair..

Plume (ploom) *noun, verb*
1. A structure or form that is like a long feather:
2. A token of honor or achievement
    The lady had a large plume in her hat.

Postponed (pohstpohnd) *adjective, verb*
1. Put off to a later time.
2. To delay until a future time
    The meeting was postponed because the speaker was late.
    The doctor had postponed all the visits that were not pressing.

Presume (prihzoom) *verb*
1. To assume, to believe something is true before you know whether or not it is.
2. Accept without verification or proof.
Synonyms: assume, imagine, suppose, think, obtrude, guess, conjecture, believe, premise, surmise, pretend
Antonyms: infer, deduce, prove, argue

Don't presume that you know everything about a person even if they are your friend.

Ravine (ruhveen) *noun*
A narrow valley that is similar to a canyon or gorge.

They found some smooth rocks in the ravine.

Repeal (rihpeel) *noun, verb*
1. An official or legal cancellation.
2. Annul by recalling or rescinding.
3. To undo a law or tax
4. To delete; an official or legal cancellation.
Synonyms: cancel, revoke, abolish
Antonyms: establish, confirm, pass, install, institute, continue, enact

I decided to repeal my offer to work on Saturday.

Replenish (reeplEHnihsh) *verb*
1. Fill something that had previously been emptied.
2. To fill something again. To resupply.
   I will have to replenish the candy dish if you keep eating the chocolate.

Responsive (rihsponsihv) *adjective*
1. Susceptible to suggestion.
2. Readily reacting to suggestions and influences.
3. Quick to react to something.
Synonyms: sensible, receptive, compassionate
Antonym: unresponsive

He was responsive to the doctor's orders to rest.
The responsive audience clapped after the exciting show.

Revere (rihvihr) *noun, verb*
To honor, to highly respect, to venerate, to regard with awe.
Antonyms: scorn, disparage

We revere Jesus as the almighty power.

Sentimental (sEHntuhmEHntuhl) *adjective*
1. Something that appeals to the emotions or romantic feelings.
2. Effusively or insincerely emotional.
3. Having or showing tender, sensitive feelings.
Antonym: unsentimental

I am a very sentimental person and I cherish the items from my grandmother.

Similar (sihmuhlur) *adjective*
Related in appearance or nature; alike though not the same.
Synonyms: alike, equivalent, corresponding, close, like, comparable
Antonyms: dissimilar, different, unlike

Purple and violet are similar colors.

Suppose (suhpohz) *verb*
1. To believe to create an idea of something.
2. To think or believe something is true.
Synonyms: expect, believe, understand, conjecture, imagine, gather, guess, think, presume

<u>Antonyms:</u> prove, demonstrate, substantiate

      I suppose that I'll be finished with my homework soon.

Suspicious (suhspihshuhs) *adjective*
1. Likely to suspect or distrust.
2. That which causes one to suspect guilt or wrong-doing.
<u>Synonyms:</u> jealous, doubtful, unsure
 <u>Antonym:</u> unsuspicious

      The police were looking for a suspicious character.

Thrive (thriiv) *verb*
1. Grow stronger.
2. Gain in wealth.
3. To survive and do well.
<u>Synonyms:</u> prosper, advance, flourish
<u>Antonyms:</u> die, fail, wane

      Savanna grasses thrive in tropical climates.

Torrid (tawruhd) *adjective*
1. Characterized by intense emotion.
2. Burning hot; extremely and unpleasantly hot.
3. Far beyond what is usual in magnitude or degree.
      We survived a torrid summer last year, but it looks like this year may be even hotter.
      Billy's infatuation with Sally led to a torrid affair.

C: Definitions

Acknowledge (aknolihj) *verb*
1. To recognize the status or rights of
2. To answer that a message was received.
3. To let someone know that one has received something
Synonyms: admit, accept, hold, allow, own, concede, consider, grant, recognize, deem, agree
Antonyms: ignore, deny, refute, reject, disclaim, neglect, disown

>He had to acknowledge that he knew me.
>The purpose for studying ancient times is to acknowledge their contributions.
>It is important to acknowledge the work of others.

Anticipate (antihsuhpayt) *verb*
1. Act in advance of; deal with ahead of time.
2. Realize beforehand.
3. Be excited or anxious about.
4. Expect questions, to look ahead at things that may happen
5. To look to the future for, to be ready for
Synonyms: prevent, foresee, expect, await, predict, forestall, see, apprehend
Antonyms: remember, recollect, remedy, recall

>I anticipate that the plane will arrive on time.
>I anticipate passing eighth-grade this time.
>Many people fail to anticipate the hidden cost when buying a car.

Aspiration (aspurayshuhn) *noun*
1. A will to succeed.
2. A strong desire to do something
Antonyms: apathy, indifference, aimlessness, dullness

>Her aspiration to be a famous doctor like Dr. Marfo will require a lot of sacrifice.
>Dr. Marfo's aspiration is to become the best internist in Charlotte.

Cautious (kawshuhs) *noun, adjective*
To be very careful and not take any chances
Synonyms: attentive, watchful, careful, wary
Antonyms: careless, rash, adventurous, temerarious

>"Please be cautious around the campfire," said Mom.
>Be very cautious when crossing the railroad tracks.
>I advised them to be cautious.

Certify (surtuhfii) *verb*
1. Officially verified
2. When someone says something is O.K.
3. Authorize officially.
4. Guarantee as meeting a certain standard.
5. To confirm as true, accurate, or genuine, especially in writing.

Synonyms: vouch, guarantee, witness, endorse, attest
Antonyms: disprove, disavow, misinform

> Could you please certify that these grades are correct?
> I can certify that this building meets county building code.

Characteristic (kEHruhkturihstihk) *noun, adjective*
1. A special or distinguishing quality.
2. A special quality or feature of something or someone.
Synonyms: quality, feature, attribute, typical, normal
Antonyms: unusual, aberrant, uncharacteristic, abstractedness

> One important characteristic of a mixture is that their compositions may vary.
> Honesty is a good characteristic.
> Good grades are characteristic STUDIOUS students.

Controversial (kontruhvurshuhl) *adjective*
1. Causing a disagreement or debate
2. Something that causes arguing about differences of opinion.
3. Something causing a disagreement, argument or a dispute.
> She discussed a controversial subject.
> The referee's decision was very controversial.

Disappoint (dihsuhpoint) *verb*   To let someone down; to not make someone proud of satisfied
Synonyms: let down, frustrate, displease, fail, sadden
Antonyms: please, satisfy, realize, justify

> Please don't disappoint me by not doing your homework.

Dissect (diisEHkt) *verb*
1. Cut open or cut apart.
2. To take something apart to analyze it
Synonyms: part, divide, slice, decompose

> I had to dissect a worm in my biology class.
> At times it can be difficult to dissect a sentence into parts of speech.

Economize (ihkonuhmiiz)
To save money; to be frugal
> In times of need, it is necessary economize in order to make ends meet.
> I was forced to economize when I lost my job.

Endanger (EHndaynjur) *verb*
Put in a dangerous, disadvantageous, or difficult position.
Antonyms: cover, defend, protect, shield

> The pollution will endanger the crops.
> Pollution can endanger wildlife.

Exemplify (ihgzEHmpluhfii) *verb*
1. Clarify by giving an example of.
2. To serve as a model or be a very good example of.

Soldier's fighting in Iraq exemplify mettlesome behavior.
We should always try to exemplify Jesus with our own actions.

Falter   (fawltur) *noun, verb*
1. To hesitate; the act of pausing uncertainly; be unsure or weak.
2. To move unsteadily or to hesitate in speaking.
Synonyms: stammer, vacillate, hesitate, waver, topple
Antonyms: proceed, run, speed, flow, discourse

>   The young child began to falter when he was learning to walk.
>   You will not falter if you know your material.
>   The music began to falter as the music box ran down.

Flourish   (flourish) *noun, verb*
1. A showy gesture.
2. To grow and succeed.
3. To grow strong, to grow abundantly, to thrive or prosper.
Antonyms: languish, fail, decline, miscarry, fade

>   She will flourish in her new environment.
>   Tomatoes will flourish in a very sunny garden if they are given water.

Fragile   (frajuhl) *adjective*
1. Vulnerably delicate.
2. Lacking solidity or strength.
3. Delicate, easily broken or damaged
Synonyms: frail, delicate, brittle, weak, feeble, breakable
Antonyms: strong, sturdy, tough, durable

>   Those dishes are very fragile and will break easily.
>   Mary's emotions are very fragile right now, and she cries easily.

Gullible   (guhluhbuhl) *adjective*
1. Easily fooled, tricked or cheated
2. Easily deceived, quick to believe
Synonyms: unsuspecting, believing, trustful
Antonyms: cynical, skeptical, astute

>   My little brother is so gullible, he believes money grows on trees.
>   He often played tricks on Tom because he was so gullible.
>   Being gullible, the young boy easily believed every word I said.

Intended   (ihntEHnduhd) *adjective*
To have in mind as a purpose or goal
>   She intended to go to the mall after school but went home instead.

Inundated   (ihnuhndaytihd)
1. Made powerless especially by too much of something
2. Overwhelmed; filled up with too much to handle.
>   The students were inundated with tons of homework for the holidays.
>   The clinic was inundated with thousands of telephone calls.

Migrate   (miigrayt) *verb*
1. Move from one country or region to another and settle there.
2. Move or travel from one country or region to another and settle there.
3. Movement of a group (people, animals or birds) from one place to another
Synonyms: emigrate, journey, move, wander, immigrate, travel

Every year, millions of monarch butterflies migrate south to wintering grounds in Mexico.
The Europeans began to migrate into America.

Negative   (nEHguhtihv) *noun, verb, adjective*
1. A reply of denial.
2. A piece of photographic film showing an image with black and white tones reversed.
3. To have bad or unpleasant feelings.
Synonyms: adverse, unfavorable, pessimistic, bad
Antonyms: positive, good

The word had a negative connotation.
That was a negative comment.

Noncommittal   (nonkuhmihtuhl) *adjective*
1. Very reluctant to give out information.
2. Unwilling to take a clear position
My uncle was noncommittal about the new seat belt law.
The noncommittal answer stalled the investigation of the theft.

Obstinate   (obstuhnuht) *adjective*
1. Difficult to manage, control, or subdue
2. Stubborn, especially in holding an attitude, opinion, or course of action
Synonyms: unruly, headstrong, stubborn
Antonyms: obedient, submissive, complaisant, pliant, amenable, yielding, pliable

Young children are often obstinate while grocery shopping with their parents.
Our boss was an obstinate person.

Peak   (peek) *noun, verb, adjective*
1. The highest point; top.
2. The pointed top of a mountain.
Synonyms: crest, crown, apogee, apex, tip, visor, top, bill, summit
Antonyms: bottom, base, foot

Tim climbed to the peak of the mountain.
We saw the eagle soar upward over the mountain peak.

Permission   (purmihshuhn) *noun*
1. Consent or approval to do something.
2. Allowing someone to do something.
Charlie asked his guardian for permission to spend the night at my house.
You should never take any medicine without the permission of your parents.
Please sign the permission slip for the field trip.

Persevere   (pursuhvihr) *verb*
1. Be persistent, refuse to stop.
2. Remaining constant to a purpose; be persistent, refuse to stop.

3. To keep going even in tough times
Antonym: give up

> To succeed, you must persevere.
> She will persevere in learning to play the piano.

Prone (prohn) *adjective*
1. Lying face downward.
2. Having a tendency (to); often used in combination.
3. Lying horizontal with the face down
4. Likely to have or do.
Synonyms: ready, horizontal, liable, inclined, obnoxious, subject, apt, flat, likely, given, open
Antonyms: vertical, upright, standing, reluctant, unlikely, erect

> All officials are supposedly human and therefore prone to error.
> Ms M is accident prone.
> When I sleep, I'm in a prone position.

Protective (pruhtEHktihv) *adjective*
1. Covering or sheilding from injury.
2. Something that helps keep things or people from being damaged, attacked, stolen, or injured.
> Wear your protective gear to fight a fire!
> A mother bear is very protective of her cubs.

Quantitative (kwontihtaytihv) *adjective*
1. Amount such as age, weight, or percent
2. Refers to amounts or numbers of things.
> "The glass holds .35 liters" is a quantitative statement.

Refusal (ruhfyoozuhl) *noun*   To say you will not do or accept something.
> Her refusal to sign the papers foregoes any acceptance of guilt of the crime.
> He is adamant in his refusal to change his mind.

Reject (rihjEHkt) *noun, verb*
1. To say no to something or someone
2. Refuse to accept.
3. Dismiss from consideration.
4. To refuse or accept, use, grant, or consider
Synonyms: veto, turn down, deny, refuse, spurn, dismiss, jettison, decline, repudiate, cast
Antonyms: accept, approve, welcome, select, appropriate, hail, choose

> He feels like a reject because his girlfriend left him.
> The Bible warns of eternal retribution for those who reject Christ.

Resume (rihzoom) *noun, verb*
1. To start or go on again after stopping.
2. Begin again; take again; occupy again
3. A summary, usually in chronological order, of your work experience.
Synonyms: proceed, reopen, begin again, continue, restart
Antonyms: discontinue, halt, stop

> The hearing was scheduled to resume next week.
> A cover letter gives a resume a more personal touch.

Retire (rihtiir) *verb*
1. Go to bed in order to sleep.
2. Withdraw from active participation.
3. Pull back or move away or backward.
4. Stop performing one's work or withdraw from one's position.
5. To give up one's job.
Synonyms: resign, give up, depart from, withdraw, exit, leave
Antonyms: advance, continue, stand, join, participate, rise

> After working at the same job for 35 years, Mr. Obeng was ready to retire.
> I usually retire to bed at nine o'clock.

Subside (suhbsiid) *verb*
1. Wear off or die down.
2. Sink to a lower level or form a depression.
3. Sink down or precipitate.
4. Grow less; die down; become less active; abate
5. To get smaller, lessen.
Synonyms: ebb, abate, wane, lessen, decrease, dwindle, diminish
Antonyms: rise, climb, grow, increase, ascend

> I hope the rain subsides before we go camping this evening.
> The pain in my head would not subside.

Supplement (suhpluhmuhnt) *noun, verb*
1. To add to or bring to completion
2. Something that completes or makes an addition <dietary supplements>
Synonyms: complement, augment, extra, addition, extend

> Exercise is a good supplement to healthy eating if you want to lose weight.
> Many people take a vitamin supplement to feel healthier.

Thriving (thriivihNG)
1. To flourish; to be successful in growth; to grow vigorously
2. Grow stronger. To flourish. Growing
> Our potato plants are thriving.
> The new baby is thriving quite well.

Thwarted (thwawrtuhd)   To keep from doing or succeeding; foil
> My sister thwarted my plans to go out last night.
> The war thwarted peace in the country.

Verbal (vurbuhl) *adjective*
1. Communicated in the form of words.
2. Of or relating to or formed from words in general.
3. Expressed in spoken words.
4. Expressed in words; not written
Synonyms: verbatim, spoken, literal, oral, unwritten, traditional
Antonyms: written, documented, inexact, vague

> Good verbal skills are an important asset during a job interview.

D: Definitions

Abhor   (abhawr) *verb*
To dislike intensely, loathe, despise
<u>Synonyms:</u> loathe, detest, scorn, disdain
<u>Antonyms:</u> admire, love, enjoy, like, adore

> I abhor laziness in anyone!
> Some people abhor green vegetables, especially spinach.

Ambidextrous   (ambuhdEHkstruhs) *adjective*
1. Able to write with both hands
2. A person who is skilled at using both their right and left hands.
> Being ambidextrous, Patrick could throw right-handed and hit left-handed.
> Ngozi is able to write with both hands. Ngozi is ambidextrous.

Arbitrary   (orbuhtrEHree) *adjective*
1. Based on chance rather than reason
2. Deciding just because you feel like it
<u>Synonyms:</u> absolute, whimsical, tyrannous, erratic, autocratic
<u>Antonyms:</u> objective, logical, lenient, mild, modest, considerate, legitimate

> Since we felt the ruling was arbitrary, we were loath to obey it.
> The captain chose his team in an arbitrary manner.

Assent   (uhsEHnt) *noun, verb*
1. To agree or express agreement.
2. To agree to something, especially after thoughtful consideration.
3. To agree or give approval.
<u>Antonyms:</u> dissent, disagree, disavowal, disagreement, difference

> When a President does not assent to legislation, he may veto the bill.
> Those with courage will not assent to actions they believe are wrong.

Bashful   (bashfuhl) *adjective*
1. Shy, not at ease, especially in a social setting
2. Someone who feels shy, especially around new people
<u>Synonyms:</u> shy, timid, reserved
<u>Antonyms:</u> forward, bold, confident, brash, unreserved, outgoing, impudent

> When I feel bashful I usually blush.

Commodities   (kuhmoduhteez)
1. Merchandise which can be sold or traded
2. Anything that is bought or sold, though the term is most often used to refer to products made from natural resources
> At the stock market people trade in commodities

Conceal   (kuhnseel) *verb*
1. Prevent from being seen or discovered.
2. To hide or keep secret, to place out of sight

3. To prevent from being seen or discovered
Synonyms: hide, cloak, mask, cover, veil, camouflage, obscure, screen
Antonyms: reveal, expose, exhibit, avow, manifest

Celebrities used to go to great extremes to conceal health problems.
The prisoner was caught trying to conceal a weapon in his shoe.
Some people go to great extremes to conceal health problems.

Defensive (dihfEHnsihv) *noun, adjective*
To be on guard against attack, be it verbal or physical
I exceeded the speed limit, so I got a ticket and had to take defensive driving.
Bill was very defensive of his ideas.

Deliberate (dihlihburuht) *verb, adjective*
1. By conscious design or purpose.
2. Discuss the pros and cons of an issue.
3. Marked by careful consideration or reflection.
4. Carefully thought out; not hasty.
Synonyms: careful, planned, thoughtful, intentional, voluntary, willful, studious, premeditated, slow
Antonyms: impulsive, spontaneous, abrupt, fast, casual, hasty, precipitate

The jury will need to deliberate for hours before giving a verdict in the criminal case.
The mean boy played a deliberate trick on the little girl.
The dance involved a deliberate exaggeration of his awkwardness.

Detest (dihtEHst) *verb*
1. Dislike intensely; feel antipathy or aversion towards.
2. When you dislike a thing or person very much.
3. To dislike strongly; to hate
Synonyms: loathe, despise, hate, dislike
Antonyms: like, love, adore

Many people detest spiders and snakes.
I detest the alarm clock when it beeps at 6 o'clock every morning.

Drastic (drastihk) *adjective*
1. Forceful and extreme and rigorous.
2. Acting rapidly or violently; extreme in effect: severe
Synonyms: radical, rash, extreme, severe
Antonyms: moderate, mild

Changing your hair color is very drastic!
These drastic measures are necessary for your success in your final exams..
The President resorted to drastic measures to curb inflation.

Elegant (EHluhguhnt) *adjective*
1. Of seemingly effortless beauty in form or proportion.
2. Stylish; rich and fine in quality
3. Tasteful, stylish, and beautiful
Synonyms: stylish, tasteful, refined, exquisite, fancy, graceful, fine
Antonyms: coarse, crude, inelegant, unsymmetrical, deformed, plain

She looked like an elegant princess in her new dress.

Candles will be the perfect complement for an elegant dinner.

Entrust   (EHntruhst) *verb*
To make someone responsible for something.
> I will entrust this money to you for safekeeping.
> I would never entrust my funds to anyone who is so slipshod in managing his own affairs.

Extravagant   (ihkstravuhguhnt) *adjective*
1. Unrestrained in especially feelings.
2. Recklessly wasteful.
3. Spending too much money, especially on luxuries.
4. Wasteful, especially with money.
Synonyms: costly, extreme, lavish, exorbitant, preposterous, wasteful, fantastic, excessive, wild, indulgent
Antonyms: economical, thrifty, sober, modest, restrained, consistent, reasonable

> Her husband bought her an extravagant birthday gift.
> I think it's extravagant to spend $500 on video game.

Extreme   (ihkstreem) *noun, adjective*
1. Existing in the greatest possible degree.
2. Farthest in any direction; very intense; radical (adj.)
Synonyms: unusual, uttermost, great, utmost, inordinate, intense, fanatic, tremendous
Antonyms: initial, primal, moderate, judicious

> He really likes extreme sports.
> The plane nearly crashed because of extreme turbulence.

Flamboyant   (flamboiuhnt) *noun, adjective*
Very colorful, showy, or elaborate
Synonyms: showy, florid, rococo, splashy
Antonyms: plain, dull

> Her costume was a flamboyant yellow.
> The flamboyant supermodel was stuck up.
> The movie star lead a flamboyant lifestyle.

Govern   (guhvurn) *verb*
1. To lead by laws or rules.
2. To be in charge of; to control or rule.
Synonyms: direct, rule, control, lead, administrate, run, manage, overrule, reign
Antonyms: follow, submit, misrule, misdirect

> You must govern your class better.
> The king had a new realm to govern.
> People who govern wickedly will not succeed.

Grievances   (greevuhnsuhz)
1. Another word for a complaint.
2. complaints about the unfair practice of Parliament
> Instead of arguing, the students discussed their grievances.
> The students filed a list of grievances because they felt mistreated.

Hazards (hazurdz)
Things that cause harm or danger
> There are many road hazards in a construction area.
> Our instructor directed us into a room where we would simulate our response to potential driving hazards.

Hectic (hEHktihk) *adjective*
1. Very busy, excited or confusing
2. Very busy, lots of things going on
Antonyms: placid, calm

> Tranquility is a rare quality in the hectic modern age.
> The last few days at school were very hectic.

Intentional (ihntEHnshuhnuhl) *adjective*
1. By conscious design or purpose.
2. To do something on purpose (when you want to do something).
Synonyms: intended, planned, deliberate, voluntary
Antonyms: accidental, unintentional, casual

> It was done with intentional harm.
> Her actions were intentional.

Legitimate (luhjihtuhmuht) *verb, adjective*
1. Make legal.
2. Authorized, sanctioned by, or in accordance with law.
3. Lawful, rightful; reasonable, justifiable
Synonyms: legal, valid, proper, justifiable, true, lawful
Antonyms: illegal, spurious, arbitrary, false, illegitimate

> You better have a legitimate reason for missing school yesterday.
> The contract on our house was legitimate.
> He had a legitimate argument.

Logical (lojihkuhl) *adjective*   Orderly and with intelligence. Make sense.
Synonyms: rational, sound, reasonable, sensible, intelligent
Antonyms: illogical, irrational, inconclusive, fallacious

> You need to give a logical explanation for your answer.
> Use your logical reasoning to make a good decision.

Mystify (mihstuhfii) *verb*
To confuse or puzzle someone.
Synonyms: confuse, baffle, bewilder
Antonyms: clarify, illuminate, explain

> I am about to mystify you with my tricks!
> Her amazing story will mystify you.

Occupations (okyuhpayshuhnz)
1. The principal activity in your life that you do to earn money.
2. Any activity that occupies a person's attention.
> He had many occupations to keep him busy.

Many occupations require more training after high school.

Petty   (pEHtee) *adjective*
1. Inferior in rank or status.
2. Contemptibly narrow in outlook.
3. Mean, small-minded, selfish
Synonyms: unimportant, paltry, casual, light, trifling, little, peanut, trivial, minor, insignificant, small,
          inconsequential
Antonyms: important, significant, tolerant, momentous, bighearted, large, generous

> People who are petty like to gossip.
> Don't let petty little problems upset you.

Pretend   (preetEHnd) *verb, adjective*
1. To give a false show in order to trick or deceive.
2. Make believe; make something up
Synonyms: pose, sham, presume, simulate, bluff, feign, imagine, claim, fantasize, fake, act
Antonyms: verify, unmask, detect

> We should never pretend to be someone that we are not.
> He tried to pretend that he hadn't heard the insult.
> Lets pretend we are a prince and a princess.

React   (reeakt) *verb*
Act in response to another action
Synonyms: recur, return, revert, reply, take, operate, respond, act, answer

> All living things react to change.
> The class did not react badly to the surprise quiz.

Rustic   (ruhstihk) *noun, adjective*
1. Characteristic of rural life.
2. Awkwardly simple and provincial.
3. A country person, especially one thought of as simple or crude.
> My mom did not want to stay in such a rustic cabin for vacation.
> The unpainted log cabin was rustic in appearance.

Sinister   (sinister) *adjective*
1. Mysteriously wicked, evil or dishonest
2. Synonyms: threatening, ominous, menacing, dire, disturbing, evil, harmful, fearful
Antonyms: benevolent, benign

> The prison camp was a very sinister place.
> The dark cave gave me a sinister feeling.

UNIT 2

Complete each sentence

Name _____   Lesson 1   Date _____

Complete each sentence.

_____   1. Patrick started to play in his desk because of **(understanding, discovered, boredom)**.

_____   2. She **(claimed, disputed, illegally)** her claim to royalty.

_____   3. He adapted to his new surroundings with minimal **(weakly, disbelieving, ease)**.

_____   4. If you park **(illegally, nimble, disbelieving)**, the police will impound your car.

_____   5. Earlier he spent 12 years in prison, much of it in **(sharp, solitary, disbelieving)** confinement.

_____   6. She become very **(claimed, weakly, alone)** when she was sick.

_____   7. She looked like an **(weariness, elegant, abruptness)** princess in her new dress.

_____   8. When you don't **(pacify, soothe, forgive)** someone, you feel bad.

_____   9. We tried to **(doubtful, agile, pacify)** the baby's crying but only her mother could calm her down.

_____   10. **(Feebly, Forgive, Disbelieving)** the old man walked to the store for food.

_____   11. My mother looked at my messy bedroom and gave a groan of **(forgive, anxious, disgust)**.

_____   12. I am **(feared, doubtful, boredom)** we will have practice today since it is raining.

_____   13. A feeling of **(weariness, disputed, feared)** came over us at the end of the mile run in P.E. class.

_____   14. Mr. Bonna sent a Valentine to his wonderful wife to show his **(affection, abruptness, boredom)**.

_____   15. His **(reluctance, discovered, abruptness)** to get on the plane was due to his fear of heights.

_____   16. The painting is very **(discovered, realistic, anxious)**.

_____   17. Why is this place so **(unruly, disorderly, weakly)**?

_____   18. Cameron is **(anxious, nicely, abruptness)** for his sister to have a baby so he can be an uncle.

_____   19. Please give your **(honest, disgust, eagerness)** and open opinion on the questionnaire.

_____   20. It is not safe to go into the jungle **(alone, clearly, feebly)**.

_____ 21. When Alex brought home his report card, he greatly **(feared, suddenness, doubtful)** his parent's discipline.

_____ 22. The athlete is **(weakly, playful, agile)** and quick.

_____ 23. I didn't hear **(ease, disagreement, clearly)** so I asked him to repeat the sentence.

_____ 24. Sometimes faint **(boredom, fatigue, praise)** is worse than no praise at all.

_____ 25. Cognition means learning and **(understanding, feared, eagerness)** something.

_____ 26. The friends of the deceased man felt very melancholy and **(sharp, playful,)**.

_____ 27. The music stopped **(clearly, agile, abruptly)**

_____ 28. He has a very **(keen, unruly, affection)** sense of humor.

_____ 29. The loud noise caused Petra to **(panic, distasteful, boredom)**.

_____ 30. Hawks have **(sharp, understanding, indifference)** talons.

_____ 31. Joshua was in a very **(playful, distasteful, disgust)** mood.

_____ 32. The illness **(indifference, feebly, proved)** to be very infectious since so many became sick.

_____ 33. Katherine has played well in recent weeks, and her **(dejection, eagerness, indifference)** was evident at her piano recital.

_____ 34. It will do no good to wrestle over this **(clearly, affection, disagreement)**.

_____ 35. Abraham Lincoln was often described as a **(elegant, reluctance, homely)** man in many ways.

_____ 36. His excuse for not doing his homework was **(agile, fatigue, disbelieving)** to his teacher.

_____ 37. I **(discovered, keen, sharp)** that ants are very smart little bugs.

_____ 38. Akua's bad temper and **(unwillingness, praise, disagreement)** to compromise caused him to be alienated from his peers.

_____ 39. During fall, I like to walk through the park and **(suddenness, admire, eagerness)** the colorful leaves.

_____ 40. Adu showed **(disagreement, unwillingness, indifference)** when it came to watching boxing.

_____ 41. She gently talked to the injured pup trying to **(soothe, reluctance, praise)** its fear.

_____ 42. All athletes must be **(alone, nimble, discovered)** in order to compete.

_____ 43. John seemed almost like a prophet with his **(insight, extent, claimed)**.

_____ 44. The **(forgive, unruly, discovered)** children were not allowed recess time.

_____ 45. They **(claimed, honest, playful)** they did not despoil the store, but they were caught on video camera.

_____ 46. That remark was crude and **(distasteful, solitary, agile)**!

_____ 47. Doing the same thing over and over is tedious, causing mental **(indifference, fatigue, homely)**.

Name _____   Lesson 2   Date _____

Complete each sentence using the words in the word list.

detrimental	celebrate	fertile	dense
optimistic	pinnacle	greedy	blunt
replenish	drenched	excite	adapt
construct	presume	lofty	core

_____ 1. The rain ____ the people waiting for the bus.

_____ 2. Using drugs is ____ to your health.

_____ 3. She is ____ about her success in school.

_____ 4. My uncle gave me some ____ advice.

_____ 5. Don't ____ that you know everything about a person even if they are your friend.

_____ 6. I will have to ____ the candy dish if you keep eating the chocolate.

_____ 7. The mantle of the earth is next to the ____.

_____ 8. Don't be ____ and eat all the cookies.

_____ 9. The flowers will thrive in the ____ soil.

_____ 10. Do not ____ the dog because he might bite you.

_____ 11. The ____ of the tower was in need of repair..

_____ 12. Memorial Day is an annual holiday that we ____ in May.

_____ 13. The smog in Louisville is very ____.

_____ 14. I know you will ____ to your new surrounding quickly.

_____ 15. Scientists use fossil records to ____ a geologic time scale.

_____ 16. The teacher has ____ goals for her students.

sentimental	insolent	similar	concise	revere
anticipate	endeavor	haughty	complex	
postponed	endanger	extreme	analyze	
exemplify	elevated	episode	torrid	

_____17. The last ____ of the story made me cry.

_____18. I am a very ____ person and I cherish the items from my grandmother.

_____19. We ____ Jesus as the almighty power.

_____20. It is not always easy to ____ what went wrong.

_____21. Be ____ when you are writing your report.

_____22. She has been ____ to manager.

_____23. The pollution will ____ the crops.

_____24. That is a ____ math problem.

_____25. I only ask that you always ____ to do your best.

_____26. Purple and violet are ____ colors.

_____27. Do you ____ what time the meeting will end?

_____28. The boy behaved like an ____ child.

_____29. Her ____ attitude did not make her a very popular girl.

_____30. He was in ____ pain.

_____31. Billy's infatuation with Sally led to a ____ affair.

_____32. Soldier's fighting in Iraq ____ mettlesome behavior.

_____33. The doctor had ____ all the visits that were not pressing.

announcement	intricate	suppose	ravine	omit
suspicious	departure	conform	formal	
responsive	indicate	thrive	barren	
conclusion	incident	repeal	plume	

_____34. The doctor told my aunt that she was ____.

_____35. David rented a tuxedo to wear to the ____ dance.

_____36. I decided to ____ my offer to work on Saturday.

_____37. I must remember to ____ my error on the final draft.

_____38. I ____ that I'll be finished with my homework soon.

_____39. The author will astound her readers with the ____ of the book.

_____40. Please ____ on the map where we are.

_____41. They found some smooth rocks in the ____.

_____42. Please affirm the ____ time.

_____43. The police were looking for a ____ character.

_____44. The ____ was greeted with happiness.

_____45. The lady had a large ____ in her hat.

_____46. The ____ audience clapped after the exciting show.

_____47. We could see many details in the ____ painting.

_____48. The sad ____ was still very vivid in his memory.

_____49. Savanna grasses ____ in tropical climates.

_____50. The new student tried to ____ to the rules of the new school.

Name _____   Lesson 3   Date _____

Complete each sentence.

_____ 1. The students were **(inundated, gullible, protective)** with tons of homework for the holidays.

_____ 2. "The glass holds .35 liters" is a **(dissect, quantitative, thwarted)** statement.

_____ 3. The war **(retire, thwarted, certify)** peace in the country.

_____ 4. At times it can be difficult to **(dissect, endanger, resume)** a sentence into parts of speech.

_____ 5. Every year, millions of monarch butterflies **(verbal, inundated, migrate)** south to wintering grounds in Mexico.

_____ 6. She **(intended, thriving, exemplify)** to go to the mall after school but went home instead.

_____ 7. I was forced to **(cautious, fragile, economize)** when I lost my job.

_____ 8. I advised them to be **(resume, cautious, retire)** .

_____ 9. The **(obstinate, noncommittal, negative)** answer stalled the investigation of the theft.

_____ 10. The hearing was scheduled to **(migrate, disappoint, resume)** next week.

_____ 11. All officials are supposedly human and therefore **(prone, characteristic, economize)** to error.

_____ 12. Many people take a vitamin **(supplement, peak, thwarted)** to feel healthier.

_____ 13. The new baby is **(thriving, permission, thwarted)** quite well.

_____ 14. Good **(verbal, acknowledge, flourish)** skills are an important asset during a job interview.

_____ 15. We should always try to **(endanger, obstinate, exemplify)** Jesus with our own actions.

_____ 16. Dr. Marfo's **(refusal, aspiration, permission)** is to become the best internist in Charlotte.

_____ 17. Tim climbed to the **(supplement, peak, falter)** of the mountain.

_____ 18. A mother bear is very **(protective, permission, intended)** of her cubs.

_____ 19. Our boss was an **(dissect, obstinate, supplement)** person.

_____ 20. She will **(characteristic, persevere, economize)** in learning to play the piano.

_____ 21. The music began to (**obstinate, falter, flourish**) as the music box ran down.

_____ 22. Tomatoes will (**thriving, flourish, thwarted**) in a very sunny garden if they are given water.

_____ 23. It is important to (**noncommittal, acknowledge, quantitative**) the work of others.

_____ 24. Could you please (**controversial, exemplify, certify**) that these grades are correct?

_____ 25. Please don't (**aspiration, dissect, disappoint**) me by not doing your homework.

_____ 26. The pain in my head would not (**verbal, resume, subside**).

_____ 27. The Bible warns of eternal retribution for those who (**falter, reject, quantitative**) Christ.

_____ 28. The word had a (**controversial, prone, negative**) connotation.

_____ 29. Honesty is a good (**characteristic, aspiration, reject**) .

_____ 30. Her (**refusal, reject, cautious**) to sign the papers foregoes any acceptance of guilt of the crime.

_____ 31. I usually (**acknowledge, thriving, retire**) to bed at nine o'clock.

_____ 32. The pollution will (**endanger, anticipate, exemplify**) the crops.

_____ 33. Mary's emotions are very (**permission, falter, fragile**) right now, and she cries easily.

_____ 34. I (**anticipate, supplement, exemplify**) passing eighth-grade this time.

_____ 35. The referee's decision was very (**controversial, quantitative, negative**) .

_____ 36. Being (**quantitative, gullible, acknowledge**) , the young boy easily believed every word I said.

_____ 37. Charlie asked his guardian for (**protective, permission, migrate**) to spend the night at my house.

Okyere Bonna, MBA

Name _____   Lesson 4   Date _____
Complete each sentence.

_____ 1. The class did not (**conceal, react, rustic**) badly to the surprise quiz.

_____ 2. The king had a new realm to (**legitimate, govern, conceal**) .

_____ 3. The President resorted to (**occupations, hazards, drastic**) measures to curb inflation.

_____ 4. He had a (**legitimate, detest, grievances**) argument.

_____ 5. Many people (**detest, grievances, arbitrary**) spiders and snakes.

_____ 6. When a President does not (**govern, assent, pretend**) to legislation, he may veto the bill.

_____ 7. People who are (**mystify, petty, extreme**) like to gossip.

_____ 8. I would never (**entrust, commodities, assent**) my funds to anyone who is so slipshod in managing his own affairs.

_____ 9. The unpainted log cabin was (**rustic, entrust, ambidextrous**) in appearance.

_____ 10. Her husband bought her an (**extravagant, bashful, rustic**) birthday gift.

_____ 11. You need to give a (**petty, occupations, logical**) explanation for your answer.

_____ 12. The prisoner was caught trying to (**drastic, conceal, defensive**) a weapon in his shoe.

_____ 13. Some people go to great extremes to (**govern, legitimate, conceal**) health problems.

_____ 14. I think it's (**logical, hectic, extravagant**) to spend $500 on video game.

_____ 15. The movie star lead a (**flamboyant, abhor, react**) lifestyle.

_____ 16. The jury will need to (**deliberate, assent, extravagant**) for hours before giving a verdict in the criminal case.

_____ 17. He really likes (**detest, extreme, commodities**) sports.

_____ 18. Many (**detest, occupations, elegant**) require more training after high school.

_____ 19. Her actions were (**elegant, arbitrary, intentional**) .

_____ 20. Don't let (**bashful, petty, sinister**) little problems upset you.

_____ 21. The plane nearly crashed because of (**arbitrary, sinister, extreme**) turbulence.

_____ 22. Ngozi is able to write with both hands. Ngozi is (**ambidextrous, hectic, intentional**) .

_____ 23. You better have a (**intentional, legitimate, entrust**) reason for missing school yesterday.

_____ 24. There are many road (**detest, hazards, arbitrary**) in a construction area.

_____ 25. The last few days at school were very (**hazards, abhor, hectic**) .

_____ 26. The dance involved a (**deliberate, elegant, logical**) exaggeration of his awkwardness.

_____ 27. Some people (**abhor, legitimate, ambidextrous**) green vegetables, especially spinach.

_____ 28. Bill was very (**defensive, occupations, react**) of his ideas.

_____ 29. Since we felt the ruling was (**entrust, petty, arbitrary**) , we were loath to obey it.

_____ 30. He tried to (**govern, pretend, petty**) that he hadn't heard the insult.

_____ 31. My mom did not want to stay in such a (**extravagant, rustic, abhor**) cabin for vacation.

_____ 32. Tranquility is a rare quality in the (**flamboyant, hectic, drastic**) modern age.

_____ 33. Being (**ambidextrous, occupations, extreme**) , Patrick could throw right-handed and hit left-handed.

_____ 34. The mean boy played a (**react, deliberate, bashful**) trick on the little girl.

_____ 35. People who (**pretend, extravagant, govern**) wickedly will not succeed.

_____ 36. We should never (**grievances, intentional, pretend**) to be someone that we are not.

_____ 37. Those with courage will not (**flamboyant, assent, logical**) to actions they believe are wrong.

_____ 38. At the stock market people trade in (**commodities, deliberate, assent**)

_____ 39. All living things (**deliberate, hectic, react**) to change.

_____ 40. Use your (**logical, extravagant, defensive**) reasoning to make a good decision.

_____ 41. It was done with (**bashful, conceal, intentional**) harm.

_____ 42. Our instructor directed us into a room where we would simulate our response to potential driving (**entrust, flamboyant, hazards**) .

_____ 43. I am about to (**mystify, elegant, drastic**) you with my tricks!

_____ 44. Celebrities used to go to great extremes to (conceal, drastic, sinister) health problems.

_____ 45. Her costume was a (pretend, conceal, flamboyant) yellow.

_____ 46. You must (defensive, sinister, govern) your class better.

_____ 47. The (sinister, logical, flamboyant) supermodel was stuck up.

_____ 48. The captain chose his team in an (grievances, arbitrary, rustic) manner.

_____ 49. The prison camp was a very (sinister, mystify, elegant) place.

_____ 50. The students filed a list of (defensive, rustic, grievances) because they felt mistreated.

_____ 51. I (deliberate, mystify, abhor) laziness in anyone!

_____ 52. The contract on our house was (abhor, ambidextrous, legitimate) .

_____ 53. He had many (occupations, commodities, intentional) to keep him busy.

_____ 54. When I feel (bashful, petty, mystify) I usually blush.

_____ 55. Lets (pretend, entrust, flamboyant) we are a prince and a princess.

_____ 56. Candles will be the perfect complement for an (elegant, mystify, extreme) dinner.

_____ 57. She looked like an (react, elegant, rustic) princess in her new dress.

_____ 58. The dark cave gave me a (legitimate, sinister, drastic) feeling.

_____ 59. These (commodities, assent, drastic) measures are necessary for your success in your final exams..

_____ 60. I exceeded the speed limit, so I got a ticket and had to take (defensive, logical, hazards) driving.

_____ 61. Her amazing story will (mystify, grievances, deliberate) you.

_____ 62. Instead of arguing, the students discussed their (arbitrary, grievances, deliberate) .

_____ 63. I will (extreme, ambidextrous, entrust) this money to you for safekeeping.

_____ 64. Changing your hair color is very (drastic, detest, extravagant) !

_____ 65. I (detest, occupations, flamboyant) the alarm clock when it beeps at 6 o'clock every morning.

UNIT 3

Match each definition with a word

Okyere Bonna, MBA

Word List

abruptness	disgust	homely	realistic
admire	disorderly	honest	reluctance
affection	disputed	illegally	sharp
agile	distasteful	indifference	solitary
alone	doubtful	insight	soothe
anxious	eagerness	keen	suddenness
boredom	ease	nicely	understanding
claimed	elegant	nimble	unruly
clearly	extent	pacify	unwillingness
dejection	fatigue	panic	weakly
disagreement	feared	playful	weariness
disbelieving	feebly	praise	
discovered	forgive	proved	

Matching

Match each definition with a word.

1. **a.** A positive feeling of liking. **b.** A feeling of kindness, fondness, love for someone or something __affection__	2. The range, distance, or space over or through which something extends. _____
3. The quality of happening with headlong haste or without warning. Sudden _____	4. **a.** Refined or tastefully lavish, excellent, splendid. **b.** Of seemingly effortless beauty in form or proportion. _____
5. Mentally quick. _____	6. Not wanting to do something _____
7. **a.** Lack of understanding or unity **b.** a quarrel; not able to come to an agreement; not of the same opinion _____	8. **a.** The feeling of having nothing to do, a tedious state **b.** The state of feeling tired, restless, and uninterested _____
9. **a.** The state of not wanting to do something. **b.** lack of enthusiasm: unwillingness or lack of enthusiasm _____	10. **a.** To be by yourself. **b.** when you are by your self _____

50

11. **a.** Great tiredness resulting from hard physical or mental work. **b.** A tired felling that lowers your level of activity. _____	12. **a.** Impossible to discipline; refusing to obey **b.** Unwilling to submit to authority. _____
13. Be uneasy or apprehensive about. _____	14. **a.** Freedom from constraint or embarrassment. **b.** Move gently or carefully. _____
15. **a.** A feeling of uneasiness. To feel worried, nervous, or eager. You may feel this before a big math test. **b.** Afraid or nervous about what may happen _____	16. **a.** Unreasonable fear causing someone to lose control **b.** Excited, scared, doesn't know what to do. _____
17. **a.** A state of melancholy depression. **b.** Lowness of spirits; sadness; depression _____	18. **a.** Cause to be more favorably inclined; gain the good will of. **b.** To make peaceful or calm; to soothe _____
19. **a.** Mentally quick. **b.** Quick in thinking and understanding. _____	20. Not having strength or sick; weak _____
21. **a.** Open to suspicion. **b.** To be unsure about something. _____	22. Not acceptable, lawful or within the law _____
23. **a.** Not pleasing in odor or taste. **b.** Unpleasant, disagreeable, objectionable or offensive _____	24. **a.** To please by praise or attention. **b.** To quiet or calm someone _____
25. **a.** To stop blaming or feeling anger toward someone; pardon or excuse. **b.** Stop blaming somebody or stop feeling angry with somebody about something. _____	26. **a.** Not attractive in appearance; plain. **b.** Unattractive, plain, simple, ordinary. _____
27. **a.** Capable of being trusted, not stealing, cheating, or lying. **b.** True to yourself and others. _____	28. **a.** The trait of remaining calm and seeming not to care; a casual lack of concern. **b.** A don't care attitude. _____
29. Clean and free from anything that makes it hard to see. _____	30. **a.** Established beyond doubt. **b.** To show that something is true or correct. _____

31. **a.** To look up to someone or something with respect **b.** Look up to with appreciation. _____	32. Full of play; fond of playing _____
33. **a.** Being real; common sense decisions **b.** Using facts and good sense to evaluate people, things, or situations; concerned with the practical; resembling real life _____	34. **a.** Clear or deep perception of a situation. **b.** The power or act of seeing into a situation. _____
35. The quality of happening with headlong haste or without warning. _____	36. Reject as false; refuse to accept. _____
37. Not in order, not disciplined _____	38. **a.** To be exhausted - very tired **b.** worn out in strength, energy, or freshness _____
39. good, pleasant, agreeable, pretty, kind, polite, etc., _____	40. **a.** Lacking companions or companionship. **b.** Without the company of others. Single, lone. Far away from society.
41. **a.** To say that something belongs to you **b.** To demand as yours or to state something strongly. _____	42. **a.** knowing what something means or how it works **b.** Appreciating the reasons for a mistake. _____
43. **a.** To honor with words or song. **b.** To say something good about something _____	44. **a.** A thin, fine edge or a pointed tip. **b.** Having a thin cutting edge or fine point. _____
45. **a.** Strong feelings of dislike. **b.** A feeling of horrified distaste for something _____	46. **a.** Find unexpectedly. **b.** See for the first time; make a discovery. _____
47. **a.** Open to debate. **b.** argued; disagreed; fought over _____	48. **a.** Having or demonstrating ability to recognize or draw fine distinctions. **b.** Intense or sharp. _____
49. **a.** A positive feeling of wanting to push ahead with something. **b.** A strong desire to do something. _____	50. Lacking physical strength or vitality. _____

Name _____   Lesson 6   Date _____

Word List			
adapt	dense	greedy	ravine
analyze	departure	haughty	repeal
announcement	detrimental	incident	replenish
anticipate	drenched	indicate	responsive
barren	elevated	insolent	revere
blunt	endanger	intricate	sentimental
celebrate	endeavor	lofty	similar
complex	episode	omit	suppose
concise	excite	optimistic	suspicious
conclusion	exemplify	pinnacle	thrive
conform	extreme	plume	torrid
construct	fertile	postponed	
core	formal	presume	

Matching

Match each definition with a word.

1. **a.** A structure or form that is like a long feather:
   b. A token of honor or achievement

   __plume__

2. Raised to a higher level.

   _____

3. Hopeful that things will turn out in the best possible way.

   _____

4. **a.** Grow stronger.
   b. Gain in wealth.

   _____

5. To show; to make known.

   _____

6. **a.** A single distinct event.
   b. An event that is unusual.

   _____

7. **a.** Say a lot with few words.
   b. Expressed in a few words.

   _____

8. **a.** A day or holiday when people do something enjoyable.
   b. To do certain things because of a special occasion.

   _____

9. To honor, to highly respect, to venerate, to regard with awe.

   _____

10. To leave, especially to go on a journey.

   _____

11. **a.** A purposeful or industrious undertaking (especially one that requires effort or boldness). **b.** Try hard; Make an effort; strive. _____	12. A sudden decline in strength or number or importance. _____
13. **a.** Showing lack of respect to rank or authority. **b.** Rude or arrogant in conduct and speech _____	14. To put in a dangerous situation; to threaten. _____
15. Wanting to have more than you need _____	16. **a.** This deepest layer is at the center of Earth. **b.** the hard center of an apple or pear _____
17. Soaked or very wet . _____	18. **a.** Of imposing height; especially standing out above others. **b.** Having or displaying great dignity or nobility. _____
19. **a.** To assume, to believe something is true before you know whether or not it is. **b.** Accept without verification or proof. _____	20. **a.** Annul by recalling or rescinding. **b.** To undo a law or tax _____
21. Related in appearance or nature; alike though not the same. _____	22. **a.** Proper and not casual. **b.** Very correct, following all the rules of conduct and/or dress _____
23. Not able to produce growing plants or crops. _____	24. A formal printed notice, as of a wedding or other event _____
25. The end of a book, play, or movie. _____	26. **a.** Readily reacting to suggestions and influences. **b.** Quick to react to something. _____
27. To illustrate or to serve as an example or by example. _____	28. **a.** The highest point; a spire **b.** A lofty peak. _____
29. **a.** Prevent from being included or considered or accepted. **b.** To leave undone or leave out. _____	30. **a.** Characterized by intense emotion. **b.** Burning hot; extremely and unpleasantly hot. _____

31. **a.** when something is very damaging to something else **b.** Anything that causes damage or injury. _____	32. **a.** Bearing in abundance especially offspring. **b.** Able to produce more, especially land that is full of nutrients. _____
33. **a.** Put off to a later time. **b.** To delay until a future time _____	34. To build something or create. _____
35. **a.** A brief section of a literary or dramatic work that forms part of a connected series. **b.** An occurrence that has happened during the course of a day. _____	36. **a.** Regard something as probable or likely. **b.** Make a prediction about; tell in advance. _____
37. **a.** To believe to create an idea of something. **b.** To think or believe something is true. _____	38. **a.** Changing to get used to something new. **b.** To adjust to a new situation or surrounding. _____
39. **a.** containing many details or small parts that are skillfully made or assembled **b.** Complicated or tangled, highly involved. _____	40. **a.** one of two ends or opposites **b.** Existing in the greatest possible degree. _____
41. **a.** Closely crowded together. **b.** very thick or crowded in space _____	42. **a.** Likely to suspect or distrust. **b.** That which causes one to suspect guilt or wrong-doing. _____
43. **a.** Make less sharp. **b.** abrupt; frank; outspoken. _____	44. **a.** Figuring out something by looking at its parts. **b.** To study carefully in order to determine what something is, what its parts are, or how its parts fit together. _____
45. **a.** Having or showing tender, sensitive feelings. **b.** Something that appeals to the emotions or romantic feelings. _____	46. A narrow valley that is similar to a canyon or gorge. _____
47. Intricate, not simple, composed of two or more related parts _____	48. **a.** Fill something that had previously been emptied. **b.** To fill something again. To resupply. _____

49. **a.** To follow an established pattern or standard **b.** To behave or think like others _____	50. Arrogant; vainly proud; showing disdain to those one views as unworthy. _____

Name _____   Lesson 7   Date _____

Word List			
acknowledge	endanger	noncommittal	resume
anticipate	exemplify	obstinate	retire
aspiration	falter	peak	subside
cautious	flourish	permission	supplement
certify	fragile	persevere	thriving
characteristic	gullible	prone	thwarted
controversial	intended	protective	verbal
disappoint	inundated	quantitative	
dissect	migrate	refusal	
economize	negative	reject	

Matching

Match each definition with a word.

1. To have in mind as a purpose or goal _intended_	2. To keep from doing or succeeding; foil _____
3. **a.** Covering or shielding from injury. **b.** Something that helps keep things or people from being damaged, attacked, stolen, or injured. _____	4. To let someone down; to not make someone proud of satisfied _____
5. **a.** To grow strong, to grow abundantly, to thrive or prosper. **b.** A showy gesture. _____	6. **a.** To hesitate; the act of pausing uncertainly; be unsure or weak. **b.** To move unsteadily or to hesitate in speaking. _____
7. **a.** Very reluctant to give out information. **b.** Unwilling to take a clear position _____	8. **a.** The highest point; top. **b.** The pointed top of a mountain. _____
9. **a.** causing a disagreement or debate **b.** Something that causes arguing about differences of opinion. _____	10. **a.** Communicated in the form of words. **b.** Expressed in words; not written _____
11. **a.** Withdraw from active participation. **b.** Stop performing one's work or withdraw from one's position. _____	12. To save money; to be frugal _____

13. **a.** A special or distinguishing quality. **b.** A special quality or feature of something or someone. _____	14. **a.** Lying face downward. **b.** Having a tendency (to); often used in combination. _____
15. To say you will not do or accept something. _____	16. **a.** To flourish; to be successful in growth; to grow vigorously **b.** Grow stronger. To flourish. Growing _____
17. **a.** officially verified **b.** Guarantee as meeting a certain standard. _____	18. **a.** Clarify by giving an example of. **b.** To serve as a model or be a very good example of. _____
19. **a.** Be persistent, refuse to stop. **b.** Remaining constant to a purpose; be persistent, refuse to stop. _____	20. **a.** Made powerless especially by too much of something **b.** Overwhelmed; filled up with too much to handle. _____
21. To be very careful and not take any chances _____	22. **a.** amount such as age, weight, or percent **b.** Refers to amounts or numbers of things. _____
23. To add to or bring to completion _____	24. **a.** A summary, usually in chronological order, of your work experience. **b.** To start or go on again after stopping. _____
25. **a.** To let someone know that one has received something **b.** To recognize the status or rights of	26. **a.** A will to succeed. **b.** A strong desire to do something
27. **a.** Vulnerably delicate. **b.** Lacking solidity or strength. _____	28. **a.** Difficult to manage, control, or subdue **b.** Stubborn, especially in holding an attitude, opinion, or course of action _____
29. Put in a dangerous, disadvantageous, or difficult position. _____	30. **a.** Consent or approval to do something. **b.** Allowing someone to do something. _____
31. **a.** Easily fooled, tricked or cheated **b.** Easily deceived, quick to believe _____	32. **a.** Realize beforehand. **b.** To look to the future for, to be ready for _____

33. **a.** Movement of a group (people, animals or birds) from one place to another **b.** Move from one country or region to another and settle there. _____	34. **a.** Cut open or cut apart. **b.** To take something apart to analyze it _____

35.   **a.** to say no to something or someone
     b. Refuse to accept.
 	
_____
	36. **a.** Sink to a lower level or form a depression.
	     b. To get smaller, lessen.
	
	_____

37. **a.** A piece of photographic film showing an image with black and white tones reversed. **b.** To have bad or unpleasant feelings. _____	

Name _____   Lesson 8   Date _____

Word List

abhor	deliberate	govern	occupations
ambidextrous	detest	grievances	petty
arbitrary	drastic	hazards	pretend
assent	elegant	hectic	react
bashful	entrust	intentional	rustic
commodities	extravagant	legitimate	sinister
conceal	extreme	logical	
defensive	flamboyant	mystify	

Matching

Match each definition with a word.

1. **a.** By conscious design or purpose. **b.** Discuss the pros and cons of an issue. <u>**deliberate**</u>	2. **a.** A country person, especially one thought of as simple or crude. **b.** Characteristic of rural life. _____
3. **a.** Based on chance rather than reason **b.** Deciding just because you feel like it _____	4. **a.** Make legal. **b.** Authorized, sanctioned by, or in accordance with law. _____
5. **a.** To prevent from being seen or discovered **b.** Prevent from being seen or discovered. _____	6. Very colorful, showy, or elaborate _____
7. Act in response to another action _____	8. **a.** To agree or give approval. **b.** To agree or express agreement. _____
9. **a.** Mysteriously wicked, evil or dishonest **b.** Synonyms: threatening, ominous, menacing, dire, disturbing, evil, harmful, fearful _____	10. To be on guard against attack, be it verbal or physical _____
11. **a.** Existing in the greatest possible degree. **b.** Farthest in any direction; very intense; radical (adj.) _____	12. **a.** Shy, not at ease, especially in a social setting **b.** Someone who feels shy, especially around new people _____

13. **a.** Merchandise which can be sold or traded **b.** Anything that is bought or sold, though the term is most often used to refer to products made from natural resources _____	14. **a.** Dislike intensely; feel antipathy or aversion towards. **b.** When you dislike a thing or person very much. _____
15. **a.** To lead by laws or rules. **b.** To be in charge of; to control or rule. _____	16. **a.** Very busy, excited or confusing **b.** very busy, lots of things going on _____
17. **a.** Another word for a complaint. **b.** complaints about the unfair practice of Parliament _____	18. To dislike intensely, loathe, despise _____
19. To confuse or puzzle someone. _____	20. **a.** Able to write with both hands **b.** A person who is skilled at using both their right and left hands. _____
21. To make someone responsible for something. _____	22. Orderly and with intelligence. Make sense. _____
23. **a.** Of seemingly effortless beauty in form or proportion. **b.** Stylish; rich and fine in quality _____	24. **a.** Recklessly wasteful. **b.** Spending too much money, especially on luxuries. _____
25. **a.** The principal activity in your life that you do to earn money. **b.** Any activity that occupies a person's attention. _____	26. **a.** Forceful and extreme and rigorous. **b.** Acting rapidly or violently; extreme in effect: severe _____
27. Things that cause harm or danger _____	28. **a.** Inferior in rank or status. **b.** Contemptibly narrow in outlook. _____
29. **a.** To give a false show in order to trick or deceive. **b.** Make believe; make something up _____	30. **a.** By conscious design or purpose. **b.** To do something on purpose (when you want to do something). _____

UNIT 4

Select the definition that most nearly defines the given word

Name _____   Lesson 9   Date _____
(Answer ID # 1083504)

Select the definition that most nearly defines the given word.

1. **disorderly**
   - Ⓐ Not good-looking. Plain and simple.
   - Ⓑ Having or showing an inclination to face facts and deal with them sensibly
   - Ⓒ Not in order, not disciplined

2. **nimble**
   - Ⓐ Find unexpectedly.
   - Ⓑ Moving quickly and lightly.
   - Ⓒ Apathy demonstrated by an absence of emotional reactions.

3. **illegally**
   - Ⓐ The opposite of awkward; graceful
   - Ⓑ Not acceptable, lawful or within the law
   - Ⓒ A feeling of horrified distaste for something

4. **distasteful**
   - Ⓐ Mentally quick.
   - Ⓑ Unpleasant, disagreeable, objectionable or offensive
   - Ⓒ Afraid or nervous about what may happen

5. **fatigue**
   - Ⓐ A thin, fine edge or a pointed tip.
   - Ⓑ Open to debate.
   - Ⓒ Great tiredness resulting from hard physical or mental work.

6. **playful**
   - Ⓐ To be exhausted - very tired
   - Ⓑ To show that something is true or correct.
   - Ⓒ Full of play; fond of playing

7. **panic**
   - Ⓐ An overwhelming feeling of fear and anxiety.
   - Ⓑ Appreciating the reasons for a mistake.
   - Ⓒ Characterized by quickness, lightness, and ease of movement; nimble. Mentally quick or alert: an agile mind.

8. **extent**
   - Ⓐ The range, distance, or space over or through which something extends.
   - Ⓑ See for the first time; make a discovery.
   - Ⓒ Having or demonstrating ability to recognize or draw fine distinctions.

9. **understanding**
   - Ⓐ Knowing what something means or how it works
   - Ⓑ Of seemingly effortless beauty in form or proportion.
   - Ⓒ Reject as false; refuse to accept.

10. **disgust**
   - Ⓐ A feeling of horrified distaste for something
   - Ⓑ The state of feeling tired, restless, and uninterested
   - Ⓒ A positive feeling of liking.

11. **proved**
   - Ⓐ Capable of being trusted, not stealing, cheating, or lying.
   - Ⓑ A feeling of uneasiness. To feel worried, nervous, or eager. You may feel this before a big math test.
   - Ⓒ Established beyond doubt.

12. **affection**
   - Ⓐ Lack of understanding or unity
   - Ⓑ Using facts and good sense to evaluate people, things, or situations; concerned with the practical; resembling real life
   - Ⓒ A feeling of kindness, fondness, love for someone or something

13. **claimed**
   - Ⓐ To demand as yours or to state something strongly.
   - Ⓑ To make less worried, pained or troubled.
   - Ⓒ The quality of happening with headlong haste or without warning. Sudden

14. **weariness**
   - Ⓐ The quality of happening with headlong haste or without warning.
   - Ⓑ Worn out in strength, energy, or freshness
   - Ⓒ to argue; to quarrel.

15. feared (A) Be uneasy or apprehensive about. (B) Clear or deep perception of a situation. (C) The feeling of having nothing to do, a tedious state	**16. indifference** (A) The trait of remaining calm and seeming not to care; a casual lack of concern. (B) Not attractive in appearance; plain. (C) Unwilling to submit to authority.
17. alone (A) Sharp and quick with the five senses; eager (B) Without other persons or things. (C) To be unsure about something.	**18. dejection** (A) Excited, scared, don't know what to do. (B) Lowness of spirits; sadness; depression (C) The power or act of seeing into a situation.
19. feebly (A) Not having strength or sick; weak (B) Truly or really; in agreement with the truth, facts, or reality. (C) Impossible to discipline; refusing to obey	**20. forgive** (A) The state of not wanting to do something. (B) Stop blaming somebody or stop feeling angry with somebody about something. (C) Open to suspicion.
21. ease (A) Having a thin cutting edge or fine point. (B) Lack of understanding or unity (C) Freedom from constraint or embarrassment.	**22. boredom** (A) A feeling of kindness, fondness, love for someone or something (B) The feeling of having nothing to do, a tedious state (C) A state of melancholy depression.
23. nicely (A) Lack of enthusiasm: unwillingness or lack of enthusiasm (B) good, pleasant, agreeable, pretty, kind, polite, etc., (C) Cause to be more favorably inclined; gain the good will of.	**24. sharp** (A) Lacking companions or companionship. (B) Having a thin cutting edge or fine point. (C) To look up to someone or something with respect
25. anxious (A) Being real; common sense decisions (B) Refined or tastefully lavish, excellent, splendid. (C) A feeling of uneasiness. To feel worried, nervous, or eager. You may feel this before a big math test.	**26. abruptness** (A) The quality of happening with headlong haste or without warning. Sudden (B) To stop blaming or feeling anger toward someone; pardon or excuse. (C) Using facts and good sense to evaluate people, things, or situations; concerned with the practical; resembling real life
27. pacify (A) A quarrel; not able to come to an agreement; not of the same opinion (B) Cause to be more favorably inclined; gain the good will of. (C) To quiet or calm someone	**28. elegant** (A) Refined or tastefully lavish, excellent, splendid. (B) When you are by your self (C) The ability to perceive the true nature of something.
29. eagerness (A) Not following rules; hard to manage (B) Quick in thinking and understanding. (C) A strong desire to do something.	**30. disagreement** (A) Unattractive, plain, simple, ordinary. (B) Lack of understanding or unity (C) Strong feelings of dislike.

31. **reluctance**
   - Ⓐ To please by praise or attention.
   - Ⓑ The state of not wanting to do something.
   - Ⓒ Intense or sharp.

32. **admire**
   - Ⓐ To be by yourself.
   - Ⓑ Argued; disagreed; fought over
   - Ⓒ To look up to someone or something with respect

33. **honest**
   - Ⓐ True to yourself and others.
   - Ⓑ Move gently or carefully.
   - Ⓒ Unreasonable fear causing someone to lose control

34. **homely**
   - Ⓐ Not attractive in appearance; plain.
   - Ⓑ To honor with words or song.
   - Ⓒ Something beautiful, suggesting great wealth.

35. **soothe**
   - Ⓐ To say something good about something
   - Ⓑ Look up to with appreciation.
   - Ⓒ Give moral or emotional strength to.

36. **unwillingness**
   - Ⓐ To say that something belongs to you
   - Ⓑ Not pleasing in odor or taste.
   - Ⓒ Not wanting to do something

37. **keen**
   - Ⓐ To make peaceful or calm; to soothe
   - Ⓑ Having or demonstrating ability to recognize or draw fine distinctions.
   - Ⓒ To find, see, or learn something, usually for the first time

38. **solitary**
   - Ⓐ Without the company of others. Single, lone. Far away from society.
   - Ⓑ A tired felling that lowers your level of activity.
   - Ⓒ Lacking physical strength or vitality.

39. **insight**
   - Ⓐ A positive feeling of wanting to push ahead with something.
   - Ⓑ Clear or deep perception of a situation.
   - Ⓒ Clean and free from anything that makes it hard to see.

40. **doubtful**
   - Ⓐ Cause to be more favorably inclined; gain the good will of.
   - Ⓑ Open to suspicion.
   - Ⓒ To find, see, or learn something, usually for the first time

41. **realistic**
   - Ⓐ Being real; common sense decisions
   - Ⓑ The trait of remaining calm and seeming not to care; a casual lack of concern.
   - Ⓒ Impossible to discipline; refusing to obey

42. **weakly**
   - Ⓐ Find unexpectedly.
   - Ⓑ Lacking physical strength or vitality.
   - Ⓒ A feeling of kindness, fondness, love for someone or something

43. **praise**
   - Ⓐ To say something good about something
   - Ⓑ The range, distance, or space over or through which something extends.
   - Ⓒ Not following rules; hard to manage

44. **unruly**
   - Ⓐ Unwilling to submit to authority.
   - Ⓑ Not having strength or sick; weak
   - Ⓒ The quality of happening with headlong haste or without warning. Sudden

45. **suddenness**
   - Ⓐ To please by praise or attention.
   - Ⓑ The quality of happening with headlong haste or without warning.
   - Ⓒ Unattractive, plain, simple, ordinary.

46. **disputed**
   - Ⓐ A don't care attitude.
   - Ⓑ Make easier.
   - Ⓒ Open to debate.

Name _____   Lesson 10   Date _____

(Answer ID # 0278320)

Select the definition that most nearly defines the given word.

1. **episode** (A) An occurrence that has happened during the course of a day. (B) Grow stronger. (C) Characterized by intense emotion.	2. **revere** (A) Adapt or conform oneself to new or different conditions. (B) To build something or create. (C) To honor, to highly respect, to venerate, to regard with awe.
3. **plume** (A) A structure or form that is like a long feather: (B) To show; to make known. (C) Hard to pass through because of dense growth.	4. **anticipate** (A) Realize beforehand. (B) Not able to produce growing plants or crops. (C) To delete; an official or legal cancellation.
5. **conform** (A) Related in appearance or nature; alike though not the same. (B) Closely crowded together. (C) Adapt or conform oneself to new or different conditions.	6. **omit** (A) Containing many details or small parts that are skillfully made or assembled (B) To leave out or unmentioned. (C) This deepest layer is at the center of Earth.
7. **endanger** (A) To survive and do well. (B) Regard something as probable or likely. (C) To put in a dangerous situation; to threaten.	8. **concise** (A) Say a lot with few words. (B) To follow an established pattern or standard (C) A part of a broadcast serial.
9. **insolent** (A) To fill something again. To resupply. (B) When something is very damaging to something else (C) Showing lack of respect to rank or authority.	10. **presume** (A) To assume, to believe something is true before you know whether or not it is. (B) A formal printed notice, as of a wedding or other event (C) Rude or arrogant in conduct and speech
11. **complex** (A) A single distinct event. (B) To assume, to believe something is true before you know whether or not it is. (C) Intricate, not simple, composed of two or more related parts	12. **similar** (A) A happening that is distinctive in a series of related events. (B) Related in appearance or nature; alike though not the same. (C) Gain in wealth.
13. **formal** (A) Expressed in a few words. (B) To adjust to a new situation or surrounding. (C) Very correct, following all the rules of conduct and/or dress	14. **sentimental** (A) Something that appeals to the emotions or romantic feelings. (B) A sudden decline in strength or number or importance. (C) Anything that causes damage or injury.

15. **drenched**
    - (A) To do something special or have festivities to observe an event or day.
    - (B) An event that is unusual.
    - (C) Soaked or very wet.

16. **blunt**
    - (A) To believe to create an idea of something.
    - (B) Anything that causes damage or injury.
    - (C) Make less sharp.

17. **exemplify**
    - (A) Realize beforehand.
    - (B) To illustrate or to serve as an example or by example.
    - (C) the innermost layer of Earth

18. **conclusion**
    - (A) The end of a book, play, or movie.
    - (B) Leave undone or leave out.
    - (C) Of imposing height; especially standing out above others.

19. **elevated**
    - (A) Raised to a higher level.
    - (B) A day or holiday when people do something enjoyable.
    - (C) That which causes one to suspect guilt or wrong-doing.

20. **construct**
    - (A) Existing in the greatest possible degree.
    - (B) To build something or create.
    - (C) Burning hot; extremely and unpleasantly hot.

21. **detrimental**
    - (A) To think or believe something is true.
    - (B) Very high or very high moral value.
    - (C) when something is very damaging to something else

22. **suspicious**
    - (A) The hard center of an apple or pear
    - (B) Likely to suspect or distrust.
    - (C) Arrogant; vainly proud; showing disdain to those one views as unworthy.

23. **departure**
    - (A) An official or legal cancellation.
    - (B) To leave, especially to go on a journey.
    - (C) abrupt; frank; outspoken.

24. **core**
    - (A) very thick or crowded in space
    - (B) Quick to react to something.
    - (C) the hard center of an apple or pear

25. **suppose**
    - (A) Bearing in abundance especially offspring.
    - (B) To believe to create an idea of something.
    - (C) Readily reacting to suggestions and influences.

26. **celebrate**
    - (A) To do something special or have festivities to observe an event or day.
    - (B) Able to produce more, especially land that is full of nutrients.
    - (C) Having or displaying great dignity or nobility.

27. **responsive**
    - (A) Susceptible to suggestion.
    - (B) A sudden decline in strength or number or importance.
    - (C) To leave undone or leave out.

28. **fertile**
    - (A) Be excited or anxious about.
    - (B) Able to produce more, especially land that is full of nutrients.
    - (C) Proper and not casual.

29. **postponed**
    - (A) Try hard; Make an effort; strive.
    - (B) A brief section of a literary or dramatic work that forms part of a connected series.
    - (C) Put off to a later time.

30. **pinnacle**
    - (A) Make a prediction about; tell in advance.
    - (B) (Architecture) a slender upright spire at the top of a buttress of tower.
    - (C) Used of a knife or other blade; not sharp.

31. **incident**
    - (A) Something that appeals to the emotions or romantic feelings.
    - (B) A single distinct event.
    - (C) Accept without verification or proof.

32. **adapt**
    - (A) Say a lot with few words.
    - (B) A token of honor or achievement
    - (C) Changing to get used to something new.

33. **ravine**
   (A) Figuring out something by looking at its parts.
   (B) Far beyond what is usual in magnitude or degree.
   (C) A narrow valley that is similar to a canyon or gorge.

34. **replenish**
   (A) To have parties or fun to enjoy a special day.
   (B) Existing in the greatest possible degree.
   (C) Fill something that had previously been emptied.

35. **endeavor**
   (A) Marked by great fruitfulness.
   (B) Prevent from being included or considered or accepted.
   (C) Try hard; Make an effort; strive.

36. **thrive**
   (A) To assume, to believe something is true before you know whether or not it is.
   (B) Grow stronger.
   (C) A purposeful or industrious undertaking (especially one that requires effort or boldness).

37. **barren**
   (A) To do certain things because of a special occasion.
   (B) Not able to produce growing plants or crops.
   (C) A lofty peak.

38. **torrid**
   (A) To illustrate or to serve as an example or by example.
   (B) Effusively or insincerely emotional.
   (C) Burning hot; extremely and unpleasantly hot.

39. **announcement**
   (A) To think or believe something is true.
   (B) Make less sharp.
   (C) A formal printed notice, as of a wedding or other event

40. **repeal**
   (A) Be excited or anxious about.
   (B) One of two ends or opposites
   (C) To undo a law or tax

41. **lofty**
   (A) To leave undone or leave out.
   (B) Of imposing height; especially standing out above others.
   (C) Complicated or tangled, highly involved.

42. **indicate**
   (A) To show; to make known.
   (B) To behave or think like others
   (C) Very high or very high moral value.

43. **intricate**
   (A) Abrupt; frank; outspoken.
   (B) Related in appearance or nature; alike though not the same.
   (C) Containing many details or small parts that are skillfully made or assembled

44. **greedy**
   (A) Having or showing tender, sensitive feelings.
   (B) To study carefully in order to determine what something is, what its parts are, or how its parts fit together.
   (C) Wanting to have more than you need

45. **dense**
   (A) A single distinct event.
   (B) Hard to pass through because of dense growth.
   (C) The end of a book, play, or movie.

46. **optimistic**
   (A) Hopeful that things will turn out in the best possible way.
   (B) A narrow valley that is similar to a canyon or gorge.
   (C) Done in a proper way. A formal letter or statement is stiff, rigid, proper, and perfect.

47. **haughty**
   - Ⓐ Arrogant; vainly proud; showing disdain to those one views as unworthy.
   - Ⓑ To study carefully in order to determine what something is, what its parts are, or how its parts fit together.
   - Ⓒ Very correct, following all the rules of conduct and/or dress

48. **analyze**
   - Ⓐ A purposeful or industrious undertaking (especially one that requires effort or boldness).
   - Ⓑ To study carefully in order to determine what something is, what its parts are, or how its parts fit together.
   - Ⓒ Rich soil that is good for growing crops.

Name _____   Lesson 11   Date _____

(Answer ID # 0773915)

Select the definition that most nearly defines the given word.

1. **prone** Ⓐ Begin again; take again; occupy again Ⓑ Lying face downward. Ⓒ To keep going even in tough times	2. **noncommittal** Ⓐ To give up one's job. Ⓑ Very reluctant to give out information. Ⓒ Amount such as age, weight, or percent
3. **disappoint** Ⓐ Stubborn, especially in holding an attitude, opinion, or course of action Ⓑ To let someone down; to not make someone proud of satisfied Ⓒ Be excited or anxious about.	4. **quantitative** Ⓐ Something causing a disagreement, argument or a dispute. Ⓑ To move unsteadily or to hesitate in speaking. Ⓒ Amount such as age, weight, or percent
5. **thwarted** Ⓐ To keep from doing or succeeding; foil Ⓑ Having a tendency (to); often used in combination. Ⓒ Movement of a group (people, animals or birds) from one place to another	6. **acknowledge** Ⓐ To let someone know that one has received something Ⓑ Realize beforehand. Ⓒ A summary, usually in chronological order, of your work experience.
7. **inundated** Ⓐ Difficult to manage, control, or subdue Ⓑ The highest point; top. Ⓒ Made powerless especially by too much of something	8. **migrate** Ⓐ Causing a disagreement or debate Ⓑ Move from one country or region to another and settle there. Ⓒ Be persistent, refuse to stop.
9. **negative** Ⓐ A piece of photographic film showing an image with black and white tones reversed. Ⓑ Sink to a lower level or form a depression. Ⓒ Refers to amounts or numbers of things.	10. **refusal** Ⓐ To say you will not do or accept something. Ⓑ Put in a dangerous, disadvantageous, or difficult position. Ⓒ Remaining constant to a purpose; be persistent, refuse to stop.
11. **anticipate** Ⓐ To start or go on again after stopping. Ⓑ To say no to something or someone Ⓒ Be excited or anxious about.	12. **certify** Ⓐ To recognize the status or rights of Ⓑ Officially verified Ⓒ To grow and succeed.
13. **cautious** Ⓐ Lacking solidity or strength. Ⓑ To take something apart to analyze it Ⓒ To be very careful and not take any chances	14. **retire** Ⓐ Pull back or move away or backward. Ⓑ Likely to have or do. Ⓒ To hesitate; the act of pausing uncertainly; be unsure or weak.
15. **dissect** Ⓐ To answer that a message was received. Ⓑ To take something apart to analyze it Ⓒ Officially verified	16. **protective** Ⓐ Refuse to accept. Ⓑ Covering or shielding from injury. Ⓒ Clarify by giving an example of.

17. **flourish**
    A To grow strong, to grow abundantly, to thrive or prosper.
    B Guarantee as meeting a certain standard.
    C Act in advance of; deal with ahead of time.

18. **falter**
    A To confirm as true, accurate, or genuine, especially in writing.
    B To move unsteadily or to hesitate in speaking.
    C Of or relating to or formed from words in general.

19. **gullible**
    A Expect questions, to look ahead at things that may happen
    B Easily deceived, quick to believe
    C Communicated in the form of words.

20. **endanger**
    A Put in a dangerous, disadvantageous, or difficult position.
    B Consent or approval to do something.
    C Very reluctant to give out information.

21. **economize**
    A Dismiss from consideration.
    B A special quality or feature of something or someone.
    C To save money; to be frugal

22. **controversial**
    A Allowing someone to do something.
    B Expressed in words; not written
    C Something that causes arguing about differences of opinion.

23. **obstinate**
    A To have bad or unpleasant feelings.
    B Stubborn, especially in holding an attitude, opinion, or course of action
    C Authorize officially.

24. **exemplify**
    A To serve as a model or be a very good example of.
    B Vulnerably delicate.
    C A reply of denial.

25. **fragile**
    A Something that helps keep things or people from being damaged, attacked, stolen, or injured.
    B Delicate, easily broken or damaged
    C To have in mind as a purpose or goal

26. **resume**
    A A summary, usually in chronological order, of your work experience.
    B Lying horizontal with the face down
    C Grow less; die down; become less active; abate

27. **thriving**
    A Withdraw from active participation.
    B To flourish; to be successful in growth; to grow vigorously
    C Something that completes or makes an addition <dietary supplements>

28. **subside**
    A To refuse or accept, use, grant, or consider
    B Sink to a lower level or form a depression.
    C Unwilling to take a clear position

29. **permission**
    A Allowing someone to do something.
    B Expressed in spoken words.
    C Cut open or cut apart.

30. **characteristic**
    A A special or distinguishing quality.
    B When someone says something is O.K.
    C Wear off or die down.

31. **aspiration**
    A Go to bed in order to sleep.
    B A strong desire to do something
    C To get smaller, lessen.

32. **reject**
    A A special or distinguishing quality.
    B Sink down or precipitate.
    C Refuse to accept.

33. **persevere**
    A To add to or bring to completion
    B Grow stronger. To flourish. Growing
    C Be persistent, refuse to stop.

34. **verbal**
    A A showy gesture.
    B Overwhelmed; filled up with too much to handle.
    C Of or relating to or formed from words in general.

35. **peak**
   Ⓐ To hesitate; the act of pausing uncertainly; be unsure or weak.
   Ⓑ The highest point; top.
   Ⓒ Communicated in the form of words.
	36. **supplement**
	   Ⓐ Something that completes or makes an addition <dietary supplements>
	   Ⓑ To move unsteadily or to hesitate in speaking.
	   Ⓒ Allowing someone to do something.

Name _____   Lesson 12   Date _____

(Answer ID # 0632822)

Select the definition that most nearly defines the given word.

1. **react** (A) Act in response to another action (B) To make someone responsible for something. (C) Synonyms: threatening, ominous, menacing, dire, disturbing, evil, harmful, fearful	2. **defensive** (A) To be on guard against attack, be it verbal or physical (B) Another word for a complaint. (C) Anything that is bought or sold, though the term is most often used to refer to products made from natural resources
3. **ambidextrous** (A) A person who is skilled at using both their right and left hands. (B) Tasteful, stylish, and beautiful (C) When you dislike a thing or person very much.	4. **occupations** (A) Any activity that occupies a person's attention. (B) Mysteriously wicked, evil or dishonest (C) To do something on purpose (when you want to do something).
5. **mystify** (A) Shy, not at ease, especially in a social setting (B) Merchandise which can be sold or traded (C) To confuse or puzzle someone.	6. **extravagant** (A) Recklessly wasteful. (B) Of seemingly effortless beauty in form or proportion. (C) By conscious design or purpose.
7. **govern** (A) Complaints about the unfair practice of Parliament (B) To lead by laws or rules. (C) To dislike intensely, loathe, despise	8. **flamboyant** (A) Very colorful, showy, or elaborate (B) Someone who feels shy, especially around new people (C) Carefully thought out; not hasty.
9. **extreme** (A) Wasteful, especially with money. (B) Farthest in any direction; very intense; radical (adj.) (C) Lawful, rightful; reasonable, justifiable	10. **abhor** (A) To dislike intensely, loathe, despise (B) The principal activity in your life that you do to earn money. (C) Existing in the greatest possible degree.
11. **deliberate** (A) Based on chance rather than reason (B) To agree or give approval. (C) Carefully thought out; not hasty.	12. **rustic** (A) Able to write with both hands (B) Characteristic of rural life. (C) Unrestrained in especially feelings.
13. **assent** (A) To agree or express agreement. (B) Dislike intensely; feel antipathy or aversion towards. (C) Discuss the pros and cons of an issue.	14. **petty** (A) Make legal. (B) Spending too much money, especially on luxuries. (C) Inferior in rank or status.
15. **commodities** (A) Things that cause harm or danger (B) Awkwardly simple and provincial. (C) Merchandise which can be sold or traded	16. **arbitrary** (A) Very busy, excited or confusing (B) Based on chance rather than reason (C) Mean, small-minded, selfish

17. **intentional**
    - (A) To hide or keep secret, to place out of sight
    - (B) By conscious design or purpose.
    - (C) To dislike strongly; to hate

18. **legitimate**
    - (A) Merchandise which can be sold or traded
    - (B) To be in charge of; to control or rule.
    - (C) Authorized, sanctioned by, or in accordance with law.

19. **detest**
    - (A) Make believe; make something up
    - (B) To dislike strongly; to hate
    - (C) Prevent from being seen or discovered.

20. **sinister**
    - (A) Mysteriously wicked, evil or dishonest
    - (B) Stylish; rich and fine in quality
    - (C) By conscious design or purpose.

21. **bashful**
    - (A) To be in charge of; to control or rule.
    - (B) Acting rapidly or violently; extreme in effect: severe
    - (C) Someone who feels shy, especially around new people

22. **conceal**
    - (A) Orderly and with intelligence. Make sense.
    - (B) To prevent from being seen or discovered
    - (C) To agree to something, especially after thoughtful consideration.

23. **grievances**
    - (A) Complaints about the unfair practice of Parliament
    - (B) Deciding just because you feel like it
    - (C) Contemptibly narrow in outlook.

24. **pretend**
    - (A) Stylish; rich and fine in quality
    - (B) Very busy, excited or confusing
    - (C) To give a false show in order to trick or deceive.

25. **drastic**
    - (A) Synonyms: threatening, ominous, menacing, dire, disturbing, evil, harmful, fearful
    - (B) Acting rapidly or violently; extreme in effect: severe
    - (C) To prevent from being seen or discovered

26. **hectic**
    - (A) very busy, lots of things going on
    - (B) Authorized, sanctioned by, or in accordance with law.
    - (C) Marked by careful consideration or reflection.

27. **entrust**
    - (A) To make someone responsible for something.
    - (B) Any activity that occupies a person's attention.
    - (C) Things that cause harm or danger

28. **elegant**
    - (A) To be on guard against attack, be it verbal or physical
    - (B) Of seemingly effortless beauty in form or proportion.
    - (C) Forceful and extreme and rigorous.

29. **hazards**
    - (A) Marked by careful consideration or reflection.
    - (B) Anything that is bought or sold, though the term is most often used to refer to products made from natural resources
    - (C) Things that cause harm or danger

30. **logical**
    - (A) Mean, small-minded, selfish
    - (B) To hide or keep secret, to place out of sight
    - (C) Orderly and with intelligence. Make sense.

UNIT 5

Choose the word that is the most nearly the same in meaning as the list of synonyms

Name _____   Lesson 13   Date _____

Choose the word that is the most nearly the same in meaning as the list of synonyms. A word should not be used more than once.

Word List

admire	disagreement	extent	nimble
affection	disgust	fatigue	praise
agile	disorderly	homely	sharp
alone	doubtful	honest	solitary
anxious	elegant	keen	understanding

1. limber, nimble, dexterous, spry _____	2. compromise, grasp, comprehension, appreciation, deal, arrangement, agreement, concept, bargain _____
3. quarrel, conflict, dispute, fight, dissension, opposition, feud _____	4. modest, unattractive, ugly, unhandsome, unbeautiful, unlovely, plain, unpretty, simple _____
5. disorganized, untidy, messy, cluttered _____	6. quick, spry, active, deft, agile, clever, sprightly, handy, adroit, brisk, lively _____
7. good, truthful, right, genuine, honorable, upright, trustworthy, sincere, conscientious _____	8. exhaustion, weakness, weariness, tiredness _____
9. abrupt, acute, keep, keen, alert, pointed, cutting _____	10. fine, exquisite, tasteful, fancy, graceful, stylish, refined _____
11. esteem, cherish, honor, consider, respect, appreciate, regard _____	12. distaste, queasiness, appall, nausea _____
13. applaud, compliments, admire, approve, laud, commendation, recommend, recognition, celebrate, compliment, commend, acclaim, hail, approval _____	14. acute, eager, sharp, ardent, avid, sensitive, fine, perceptive _____

15. fearful, breathless, impatient, uneasy, aghast, worried, apprehensive, ardent, eager, nervous _____	16. attachment, feeling, love, devotion, emotion, fondness, tenderness, warmth _____
17. apart, lone, unaccompanied, solitary, isolated, unparalleled, lonesome, secluded, unaided, solo, removed, unattended _____	18. isolated, lone, single _____
19. improbable, unlikely, questionable, dubious, uncertain, impossible _____	20. radius, proportion, measure, extension _____

Name _____   Lesson 14   Date _____

Choose the word that is the most nearly the same in meaning as the list of synonyms. A word should not be used more than once.

1. costly, indulgent, wild, wasteful, lavish, fat, undue, excessive, preposterous, unconscionable, dear, fantastic, exorbitant, excessive, great _____	2. respond, operate, reciprocate, recur, act, return, revert, answer, take, work, function, operate, reply, answer _____
3. lawful, legal, sensible, proper, verbatim, valid, lawful, true, justifiable, authoritative _____	4. presume, profess, claim, act, aim to, simulate, fantasize, play, affect, pose, assume, presume, counterfeit, fake, imagine _____
5. great, intense, tremendous, bizarre, furious, fanatic, utmost, uttermost, unusual, abnormal, big talk, extravagant, immoderate _____	6. heat, frenetic, rubicund, fire _____
7. authorize, give in charge, extend credit, hand _____	8. peanut, trifling, casual, small, light, insignificant, deaf to reason, minor, paltry, unimportant, inconsequential, authoritarian, trivial, hidebound, little, paltry _____
9. potent, rigorous, extreme, radical, virulent, rash, desperate, severe _____	10. studious, uncommunicative, indolent, ponder, slow, thoughtful, careful, intentional, willful, speculate, planned, voluntary, premeditated _____
11. of design, voluntary, intended, willful, deliberate, conscious, planned, voluntary _____	12. tyrannous, absolute, erratic, subjective, chance, summary, unguarded, autocratic, wayward, capricious _____
13. uncultivated, peasant, farm, unsophisticated _____	14. timid, reserved, shy, withdrawn, meek, incompatible, cool _____
15. luxurious, chic, fancy, pleasant, stylish, excellent, graceful, exquisite, tasteful, fine _____	16. screen, envelop, veil, mask, cover, cloak, file and forget, curtain, hide, ensconce _____
17. reasonable, valid, sound, sufficient, legitimate, intelligent, sensible, rational, sober _____	18. dislike, loathe, hate, despise _____

19. disapprove of, scorn, loathe, scorn, detest, detest, disdain, dislike	20. shifty, malign, ill, not easy
_____	_____

Name _____   Lesson 15   Date _____

Choose the word that is the most nearly the same in meaning as the list of synonyms. A word should not be used more than once.

Down

1. pose, feign, sham, simulate, fantasize, act, presume, imagine, claim, fake, bluff
2. screen, camouflage, cover, veil, cloak, hide, obscure, mask
4. utmost, inordinate, intense, fanatic, great, unusual, uttermost, tremendous
5. showy, rococo, ornate, ostentatious
10. return, take, operate, recur, reply, respond, act, revert, answer

Across

3. despise, loathe, dislike, hate
6. tyrannous, autocratic, absolute, wayward, whimsical
7. planned, thoughtful, careful, premeditated, willful, voluntary, intentional, slow, studious
8. trifling, trivial, light, insignificant, small, minor, little, peanut, casual, inconsequential, unimportant, paltry
9. confuse, baffle, bewilder
11. valid, legal, lawful, justifiable, true, proper

UNIT 6

Choose the word that is the most nearly the same in meaning as the list of synonyms

Name_____ Lesson 16 Date _____

Synonyms (Answer ID # 0453315)

```
D L Y Y L I T E A S E L U F A L P E U T P D I M
T A E E L U L G W N O E A G E R N E S S E E A D
V E D O L R F S I E T A P I N O C U S N E T S H
D L I D I T E Y N S A C U P L T N O N L F T H Y
L R S I F N T D A A N R C A K I P R E H S U U N
U U P S E E E N R L E I I E H D E V A R P P N T
F D U T C M D T E O P K E N Y W E I E V R S E E
E R T A N E D N N G S N I E E D N A A O L I E S
T W E S A E G N I V E I L E B S I D V T C D R E
S A D T T R D L N I D L D G I E S E Y N I I H R
E S I E C G D S S E N R E G E A D A I A N E I U
T H A F U A L A N E I F H U S A P E S G A R W N
S I K U L S R E L U C T A N C I U S O E P L A S
I D S L E I R S O L I T A R Y V D O B L E Y V H
D E D A R D S R L A E S E T S E N O H E E E R S
P A C I F Y S H A R P T N E M E E R G E S I D N
I F I T U E R R N N A P R L N T E T C M T N K I
```

Choose the word that is the most nearly the same in meaning as the list of synonyms. Then find the correct form in the word search.

1. divergence, opposition, conflict, feud, dissension, quarrel, negative, noncompliance, fight, dispute, departure pesuhfii suddenneess suddenness solitary disagreement understanding soluhtihree disagreament pacify	2. pointed, bleak, abrupt, dishonest, cutting, acute, attentive sharp nible agile praise extent shar eguli axtent nimble
3. objection, deliberation, passive resistance, resistance aegerness kuen disputed eagerness keen disputed disbeleving disbelieving reluctance	4. reputable, unrestrained, true, genuine, just, good, right, upright, scrupulous, real, unfeigned, worthy, fair, sterling dejection deection honest soothi soothe insigt insight weariness wihreanuhs

5. cluttered, variable, revolutionary, unmanageable, untidy, messy, indecisive, disorganized

forgiv	forgive
indiifference	disorderly
doubtful	indifference
alone	dissorderly
uhlon	

6. tested, veritable, fixed, not in error

provved	affection
uffectoon	proved
realistic	ehluhguht
disust	elegant
disgust	

7. unpalatable, nasty, odious, tasteless

nicely	anxious
distastiful	unruly
humely	distasteful
homely	anxios
nicily	

8. abject fear, trepidation, awe, alarm, nervousness, fright, distress, consternation, scream, dismay, howl, fear, dread, riot, terror, stampede

admire	panic
wealy	paniic
clearly	idmare
weakly	playful
clealy	

9. confounded, upset, moot, suspect

disasteful	fatigue
forgive	eezz
distasteful	ease
daspited	disputed
fargive	

10. foresight, providence, penetration, appreciation

ease	admire
kean	insight
insigt	ee
keen	reluctance
admier	

11. stupor, torpor, heaviness, apathy

wihreanuhs	disorderly
disputed	disordely
panic	honest
duspotid	weariness
hanest	

12. extenuate, repose, leisure, forward, relaxation, comfort, clear, spontaneity, rest, gentle, soothe, easement, prosperity

priase	praise
suddenness	undestanding
ee	alone
uhlahn	understanding
ease	

13. acute, sharp, eulogy, perceptive, deep, agile, eager, sensitive, fine, alert, avid, ardent

playful	exten
playfu	keen
pacify	distastiful
pasuhfii	extent
distasteful	

14. curiosity, promptness, accord, prejudice

fatigue	fuhteag
elegent	eagerness
elegant	unruly
disagreement	disagreament
unruy	

15. relieve, arrange, lull, smooth hamely pacify soluhtehrea weakly nihbuhl wieklee nimble homely solitary	16. aloof, lone, insular, particularly, detached, removed, isolate, only, only, unaided, singular, lonesome, matchless, unattended boredom agil boridom dusgust alane alone disgust agile soothe
17. single, secluded, separate, removed, withdrawn, lone, isolated raelistic indifferince realistic solitary niisle indifference disbelieving nicely soltary	18. atheist, without faith, heathen, skeptical sherp sharp nihmuhl fargive disbelieving nimble disbeleiving anxious forgive
19. barbaric, tasteful, choice, exquisite, refined, fancy, fine, graceful, princely, advantageous elegant disgust fatigue doubtful elegent disagreement dosugriement fetigeu duobtul	20. energetic, humorous, amusing, lively, vital, frisky, joking, impish, hearty, frolicsome enruly playful disorderly honest affection unruly honist afection disordely

Name _____   Lesson 17   Date _____

Synonyms: Choose the best group of words similar in meaning to the given word

(Answer ID # 0654047)

1. _____ distasteful

a. exactly, strictly, right, in detail

b. approve, soap, approval, credit, extol, laud, commendation, recognition, compliments, applaud, bless, compliment, compliment, hail, bless, recommend

c. acuity, penetration, providence, note

d. tasteless, repugnant, nasty, uncongenial

e. wicked, amusing, frisky, joking, frolicsome, frisky, roguish, energetic, lively, skittish

2. _____ disgust

a. order, reach, continuum, territory, extension, point, matter, sweep, size, magnitude

b. lull, rank, hush, wane

c. acquit, condone, decontaminate, clear, melt, absolve, spare

d. distemper, disease, warmth, emotion, devotion, love, tenderness, ill, fondness, emotion, attachment, feeling

e. nausea, queasiness, distaste, give offense, repulse, distaste, appall, antipathy

3. _____ unruly

a. irreligious, heathen, unconfident, atheist

b. raucous, rowdy, uninhibited, disorderly, recalcitrant, turbulent, unmanageable, indomitable, irrepressible, boisterous, wild, uncontrollable, disobedient, uncooperative, revolutionary

c. reckless, nimble, fleet, precipitate, supple, dexterous, limber, spry

d. fancy, pleasing, graceful, princely, exquisite, tasteful, nice, fine, stylish, noble

e. shy, howl, terror, fright, scream, distress, trepidation, fear, alarm, dread, bear panic, horror, point, riot, frenzy, dismay

4. _____ praise

a. approve, soap, approval, credit, extol, laud, commendation, recognition, compliments, applaud, bless, compliment, compliment, hail, bless, recommend

b. diarrhea, pessimism, movement, obsession

c. determined, in the bag, unquestionable, historical

d. reduction, exhaustion, weariness, dysentery, tiredness, exhaust, weakness, diarrhea

e. scrupulous, good, decent, upright, verbatim, real, straightforward, candid, genuine, conscientious, true, genuine, right, uninhibited

5. _____ understanding

a. torpor, lassitude, mental strain, heart strain

b. quick, sprightly, spry, attentive, handy, clever, lively, adroit, active, brisk, deft, agile, precipitate, active, vigilant

6. _____ panic

a. conflict, dispute, quarrel, opposition, variety, fight, dissension, feud, opposition, deviation, distaste

b. single, isolated, all alone, any, one, nonconformist, lone

c. unostentatious, garden, unhandsome, unpretentious, unattractive, roomy, dry, unbeautiful, dull, ugly, unpretty, unlovely, plain, indivisible

d. appreciation, agreement, comprehension, grasp, amity, deal, enlightenment, brotherly love, compromise, concurrence, bargain, arrangement, concept

e. leaning, consent, accord, bent

c. shy, howl, terror, fright, scream, distress, trepidation, fear, alarm, dread, bear panic, horror, point, riot, frenzy, dismay

d. stand, distaste, lack of enthusiasm, electric resistance

e. avid, apprehensive, disturbed, grim, ardent, impatient, keen, nervous, aghast, worried, ardent, eager, eager, uneasy, fearful

7. _____ weakly

a. unqualified, sincere, empirical, literal

b. inattention, inertia, lackluster, detachment, apathy, nonchalance, inferiority, disregard

c. alert, acute, sharp, eager, avid, acute, sensitive, caustic, ardent, fine, perceptive, exclaim

d. not hardly, bloodless, flaccid, low

e. defer to, consider, respect, appreciate, regard, cherish, esteem, honor, honor, endorse, deify

8. _____ forgive

a. detached, just, isolate, unique, unattended, removed, lonesome, singular, solo, aloof, apart, but, apart, unique

b. upset, confounded, suspect, moot

c. impossible, uncertain, problematic, improbable, dishonest, thick, devious

d. prosperity, relaxation, freedom, gracefulness, leisure, relief, spontaneity, composure, rest, soothe, repose, flow, comfort

e. acquit, condone, decontaminate, clear, melt, absolve, spare

9. _____ indifference

a. promptness, alacrity, impatience, speed

b. inattention, inertia, lackluster, detachment, apathy, nonchalance, inferiority, disregard

c. obscure, messy, cluttered, unorthodox, untidy, different, inconstant, disorganized

d. torpor, lassitude, mental strain, heart strain

e. raucous, rowdy, uninhibited, disorderly, recalcitrant, turbulent, unmanageable, indomitable, irrepressible, boisterous, wild, uncontrollable, disobedient, uncooperative, revolutionary

10. _____ ease

a. prosperity, relaxation, freedom, gracefulness, leisure, relief, spontaneity, composure, rest, soothe, repose, flow, comfort

b. not hardly, bloodless, flaccid, low

c. unqualified, sincere, empirical, literal

d. impossible, uncertain, problematic, improbable, dishonest, thick, devious

e. distemper, disease, warmth, emotion, devotion, love, tenderness, ill, fondness, emotion, attachment, feeling

Name _____   Lesson 18   Date _____

Synonyms
(Answer ID # 1043575)

1. _____ endeavor	2. _____ drenched
a. desolate, unproductive, uncultivated, impotent, effete, vacant, bare, sterile, inane, impotent, unfertile, empty, infertile	a. lift, invalidate, revoke, abolish, nullify, cancel, abolish
b. strive, job, attempt, undertake, seek, try, strain, seek, deed	b. design, incident, secondary plot, switch, parenthesis, event, development, occurrence
c. arouse, stimulate, generate, inspire, provoke, perturb, motivate, prime, stir, interest, inspire, rouse, instigate, agitate, thrill, pique	c. happy, swollen, gay, mellow
d. affect, hint, reveal, show, mark, imply, testify, point out, attest, suggest, dramatize, wave, betoken, spotlight, designate	d. fabricate, pyramid, raise, assemble, produce, form, manufacture, incorporate, shape, establish, compose, frame, build, make
e. unsure, unethical, queer, rotten, uncertain, jealous, problematic, apprehensive	e. reconvert, recruit, return, subsidize
3. _____ episode	4. _____ endanger
a. suit, comply with, agree, observe, obey, fit, lock, go, square, suit, adjust, follow, accommodate with, attune	a. pagoda, extreme, all, sky
	b. vouch, stand, say, bulletin
b. benevolent, grand, towering, reasonable, overbearing, tall, high, visionary, elevated, haughty, proud, contemptuous, arrogant	c. compassionate, giving, irritable, sensible, reflex, receptive, pliable, susceptible
c. design, incident, secondary plot, switch, parenthesis, event, development, occurrence	d. menace, incur danger, peril, imperil
d. gather, flourish, advance, develop, succeed, flower, prosper	e. improvident, cavalier, rude, saucy, lofty, uncourteous, discourteous, impertinent, impudent, overbearing
e. deadly, deleterious, mischievous, lethal, unfavorable, ill, adverse, contrary, negative, difficult	
5. _____ conclusion	6. _____ celebrate
a. diamond, bead, manicure, paint	a. thunder, herald, observe, cry, lionize, keep, blazon, honor
b. sophisticated, complicated, difficult, composite, hard, elaborate, intricate, knotty, compound, involved, intricate, compound, composite, confused	b. passage, furrow, cut, gully
	c. fervid, passionate, humid, fiery

c. knotty, elaborate, conglomerate, patchy, knotty, varied, detailed, complicated, involved, sophisticated, complex, fancy

d. solemn, explicit, ceremonious, set, extrinsic, proper, ceremonious, nominal, stately, conventional, regular, official

e. lineage, finish, mystique, stop, proposition, termination, maturity, end, cease, finale, close, inference, cessation, judgment, deduction

d. story, twist, experience, movement, event, affair, scheme, happening

e. evaluate, discuss, list, inspect, investigate, study, infer, examine

---

7. _____ extreme

a. ample, bountiful, wholesale, fat, productive, fruitful, rich, abundant

b. fanatic, caricature, tremendous, great, unusual, uttermost, intense, apex, dizzy, utmost, immoderate, outstanding, fierce

c. intercept, see, await, foresee, apprehend, prevent, predict, await, herald, divine, expect, forestall, foresee

d. magnify, deify, enjoy, favor

e. name, free, typify, shadow

8. _____ core

a. kernel, seed, essence, center, purport, essence, downtown, middle, nut, foundation, gist, burden, midst, upshot

b. arrogant, prominent, vain, conceited, complacent, ethereal, lofty, proud

c. pretend, guess, believe, guess, expect, suspect, think, understand, conjecture, connote, presume, be afraid, imagine, infer, take

d. correspond, fit, conform, tailor, vary, change, discipline

e. pleasant, radiant, hopeful, confident, irrepressible, trusting, positive, blithe

---

9. _____ incident

a. slight, rescind, reject, expurgate, neglect, forget, exclude

b. close, analogous, equivalent, mock, like, corresponding, following, alike, comparable

c. full, sturdy, compact, tight, thick, dull, stupid, tight, close, dumb, opaque

d. brief, direct, condensed, succinct, synoptic, brief, succinct, short

e. story, twist, experience, movement, event, affair, scheme, happening

10. _____ exemplify

a. ravenous, selfish, avaricious, mercenary, desirous, venal, voracious, acquisitive

b. leaving, diversion, going, sweep, variation, exit, diversity, release, divergence, deviation, exodus, withdrawal

c. premise, infringe, hope, postulate, postulate, believe, surmise, imagine, attempt, conjecture, think, guess, assume, pretend, suppose, intimate

d. name, free, typify, shadow

e. slight, rescind, reject, expurgate, neglect, forget, exclude

Name _____   Lesson 19   Date _____

Synonyms
(Answer ID # 0800933)

1. _____ gullible	2. _____ migrate
a. bill, acme, tip, crown, top, summit, crest, mountain, visor	a. attentive, wary, watchful, careful
b. weak, breakable, delicate, feeble, frail, brittle	b. wander, travel, immigrate, emigrate, journey, move
c. resign, depart from, give up, exit, withdraw, leave	c. predict, await, forestall, prevent, foresee, apprehend, see, expect
d. decompose, sever, cleave, separate	d. restart, proceed, continue, reopen, begin again
e. unsuspecting, believing, trustful	e. unruly, headstrong, stubborn
3. _____ dissect	4. _____ disappoint
a. feature, quality, normal, typical, attribute	a. pessimistic, unfavorable, bad, adverse
b. wane, diminish, ebb, lessen, abate, decrease, dwindle	b. repudiate, veto, spurn, shed, refuse, scrap, turn down, dismiss, deny, disapprove
c. decompose, sever, cleave, separate	c. witness, vouch, endorse, attest, warrant
d. horizontal, likely, subject, liable, apt, ready, obnoxious, flat, inclined, susceptible, given	d. addition, augment, extra, extend, complement
e. literal, oral, verbatim, unwritten, traditional, spoken	e. displease, fail, sadden, let down, frustrate
5. _____ fragile	6. _____ subside
a. wane, diminish, ebb, lessen, abate, decrease, dwindle	a. agree, recognize, admit, hold, deem, own, consider, grant, concede, allow, accept
b. witness, vouch, endorse, attest, warrant	b. decompose, sever, cleave, separate
c. unruly, headstrong, stubborn	c. resign, depart from, give up, exit, withdraw, leave
d. weak, breakable, delicate, feeble, frail, brittle	d. displease, fail, sadden, let down, frustrate
e. horizontal, likely, subject, liable, apt, ready, obnoxious, flat, inclined, susceptible, given	e. wane, diminish, ebb, lessen, abate, decrease, dwindle

7. _____ falter	8. _____ retire
a. literal, oral, verbatim, unwritten, traditional, spoken	a. attentive, wary, watchful, careful
b. addition, augment, extra, extend, complement	b. feature, quality, normal, typical, attribute
c. topple, hesitate, vacillate, stammer, waver	c. resign, depart from, give up, exit, withdraw, leave
d. predict, await, forestall, prevent, foresee, apprehend, see, expect	d. pessimistic, unfavorable, bad, adverse
e. weak, breakable, delicate, feeble, frail, brittle	e. bill, acme, tip, crown, top, summit, crest, mountain, visor
9. _____ obstinate	10. _____ reject
a. restart, proceed, continue, reopen, begin again	a. horizontal, likely, subject, liable, apt, ready, obnoxious, flat, inclined, susceptible, given
b. unruly, headstrong, stubborn	b. restart, proceed, continue, reopen, begin again
c. bill, acme, tip, crown, top, summit, crest, mountain, visor	c. repudiate, veto, spurn, shed, refuse, scrap, turn down, dismiss, deny, disapprove
d. attentive, wary, watchful, careful	d. predict, await, forestall, prevent, foresee, apprehend, see, expect
e. witness, vouch, endorse, attest, warrant	e. resign, depart from, give up, exit, withdraw, leave

UNIT 7

Choose the word similar in meaning to the given group of words

Name _____ Lesson 20 Date _____

Synonyms: Choose the word similar in meaning to the given group of words

(Answer ID # 1092820)

1. sensitive, level, bent, inclined, subject, sensitive, horizontal, likely, ready, apt, leaning, open, flat, given, liable, obnoxious pronne protective inundated disappoint protectivi prone inundatted deseppoint controversial	2. sodden, cut up, stricken, undone fregile exempify sobsade fragile subside persevere inundated inundatted exemplify
3. reopen, restart, begin again, annals, obituary, continue, recital, proceed, restatement entihsuhpayt resume rsume flouris retire flourish peak anticipate rihtiir	4. metric, an, certain, any acnowledge rejec thwartid acknowledge quantitative thwarted verbal reject virbal
5. recognize, own, allow, accept, accept, swear, admit, reply, agree, deem, concede, admit, hold, consider, grant negative cautious acknowledge uknalahj characteristic falter characteristec faltor negativi	6. preservative, conservative, vigilant, guardian obstinate obtuhnuht espiration protectiive rifusal protective aspiration gullible refusal
7. fall, lessen, ebb, progress, dwindle, decrease, abate, stir, rise, diminish, wane supplement suside permission endangor migrate subside suplement endanger pormissien	8. compromise, hazard, encounter danger, menace persevere gullible endangor gullibli obstinate obtuhnuht pursuhihr cautious endanger
9. unsound, womanish, breakable, delicate, frail, feeble, brittle, weak, thin, wispy anticipate permission retire refual fragile permisseon retre frigali refusal	10. guarantee, sanction, vouch, reassure, verify, witness, permit, approve, document, attest negativi aknollihj negative diisekt inundated inundatted certify dissect Acknowledge

11. honest, natural, oral, unwritten, vocal, spoken, traditional, correct, verbatim, literal		12. bad, discordant, antagonistic, abrogate, unfavorable, at variance, adverse, pessimistic	
peak	virbul	noncommittal	nihguhtihv
triving	thriving	intende	contrroversial
faltir	verbal	controversial	exemplify
falter	reject	negative	intended
rejict		exemlify	

13. wary, on guard, cool, watchful		14. lagniappe, blow, evidence, device	
protective	potective	fluorish	prone
fourish	disappoint	endanger	thwartted
ospiratien	dihsuhpiont	endangor	resumi
noncommittal	flourish	resume	flourish
aspiration		thwarted	

15. compliance, accord, license, leniency		16. divine, visualize, see, antedate, visualize, predict, foresee, await, prevent, expect, nullify, forestall, think	
quantitative	resume		
flourish	quantitateve	refusal	anticiate
cirtify	flurish	negative	anticipate
permission	certify	nigitive	miegrayt
resuume		migrate	intended
		rifasal	

17. bill, point, crest, top, summit, assimilation, vertex, pink, visor, meridian, pitch, crown, tip, acme		18. baffle, sadden, tantalize, let down, frustrate, displease, fail, thwart, bilk	
peak	prone	noncommittal	pratective
paek	ostuhnuht	disappoent	permission
acknowledge	proohn	permissoin	protective
obstinate	qauntitative	disappoint	verbal
quantitative		noncommitta	

19. problematic, questionable, quarrelsome, debatable		20. spurn, decline, refuse, dismiss, disapprove, dismiss, turn down, forbid, cast, jettison, waive, veto, discard, decline, deny, repudiate	
fregile	thriving		
supplement	fragile	falter	endanger
triving	cantroversial	subside	guhluhbuh
rejject	reject	gullible	falte
controversial		rejet	reject
		subsidi	

Name _____   Lesson 21   Date _____

Synonyms: Choose the word similar in meaning to the given group of words

(Answer ID # 0193394)

1. deliberate, planned, voluntary, of design, knowing, on purpose, intended, voluntary intentional rusticc rustic extravagant legitimate legitimaate arbitray arbitrary etravagant	2. gaudy, ostentatious, showy, showy, rich, pedantic, ornate, splashy, rococo, splashy drasti entrust flamboyant bashful exreme basful drastic etrust extreme
3. weighty, intelligent, rational, rational, sensible, good, sound, reasonable, consistent ulegent deliberate logical elegant abhor ambidexrous abher lojikuhl ambidextrous	4. assume, pose, claim, simulate, fantasize, venture, imagine, simulate, act, presume, appropriate, affect, counterfeit, cover up, fake pritend petty assent defeensive assint pretend sinister pett defensive
5. legal, unfictitious, justifiable, natural, substantial, lawful, valid, weighty, proper, true conceal raect ditest hectic concal legitimati legitimate detest react	6. severe, yeoman, rural, sober ambidextrous rusti rustic intentional etreme sinister siniter ombadextreos extreme
7. covering, guardian, watchful, parental govern drastic difensive goern dratic deliberate deliberete defensive petty	8. imperfect, small, insignificant, evasive, inconsequential, peanut, minor, light, trifling, casual, paltry, little, trivial, grave, deficient, unimportant hictic hectic legitimate pehte petty abhor flamboyant legitimatee Flamboyant
9. rash, fierce, severe, Draconian, intense, extreme, immoderate, radical entrust mystify drostic drastic pretend mystif elegant entust elegent	10. stylish, laudable, proud, exquisite, refined, polished, graceful, direct, fine, fancy assent rusti loggical logical assint extravagant extavagant elegant Rustic

11.	screen, eclipse, mask, camouflage, distract attention from, obscure, screen, cover, hide, stash	12.	meticulous, intentional, studious, slow, moderate, thoughtful, planned, careful, willful, premeditated, debate, studious, voluntary

conceal	deffensive
defensive	abhor
react	abher
deliberate	reat
concaell	

detest	deliberate
erbitrary	mystify
ditest	logical
deliberati	arbitrary
mihsuhfii	

13.	shy, nervous, sheepish, cool, backward, reserved, timid	14.	excited, fever, burnt, wild

petty	cencoel
govern	pety
conceal	bashful
basful	flamboyant
flaamboyant	

extavagant	ambidetrous
etrust	extravagant
hictic	hectic
entrust	ambidextrous
rustic	

15.	answer, take, act, revert, answer, perform, return, function, function, respond, recur, operate, retort, reply	16.	take, correspondence, cohere, receive

eleant	sinistor
react	intentional
pretend	pretind
elegant	sinister
raect	

extreme	hectic
assent	uhseht
drasticc	luhjihtuhuht
exteme	drastic
legitimate	

17.	flexible, shifty, generally capable, false	18.	carry authority, handle, pull, restrain, withhold, repress, direct, overrule, lead, run, render, dominate

ambidetruos	abhor
deliberete	pretend
pritend	sinister
ambidextrous	deliberate
sinnister	

govern	logical
rustic	arbitrary
lagical	rusti
elegant	erbitrary
llegant	

19.	wasteful, excessive, indulgent, grotesque, preposterous, wild, impractical, fantastic, dizzy, unconscionable, lavish, bounteous, undue, costly, improvident	20.	disdain, detest, scorn, be hostile to, loathe, disdain, loathe, not care for

etrust	intentional
flambooyant	bashful
intentionel	entrust
bahful	flamboyant
extravagant	

legitimate	difensave
defensive	legitemate
mystify	abher
abhor	mihtuhfii
detest	

UNIT 8
Pick the word that completes the second pair with the same relationship.

Name _____   Lesson 22   Date _____

(Answer ID # 0272867)

Study the relationship between the first set of words. Pick the word that completes the second pair with this same relationship.

1. conceal : _____ :: baffle : confuse

   Ⓐ appear   Ⓑ fire   Ⓒ hide   Ⓓ review

2. sleep : doze :: awaken : _____
   Ⓐ mystify   Ⓑ rouse   Ⓒ fluster   Ⓓ wince

3. without giving up : relentlessly :: on purpose : _____

   Ⓐ mournfully   Ⓑ vigorously   Ⓒ grudgingly   Ⓓ deliberately

4. quick and light : nimble :: thick : _____

   Ⓐ crass   Ⓑ foul   Ⓒ dense   Ⓓ drastic

5. commodities : products :: alternatives : _____
   Ⓐ promises   Ⓑ options   Ⓒ requirements   Ⓓ strengths

6. elegant : graceful :: dainty : _____

   Ⓐ flexible   Ⓑ soft   Ⓒ delicate   Ⓓ decorated

7. naturally, without thought : instinctively :: without purpose : _____

   Ⓐ intently   Ⓑ collectively   Ⓒ drastically   Ⓓ aimlessly

8. quick : slow :: kind : _____
   Ⓐ unyielding   Ⓑ obstinate   Ⓒ merciless   Ⓓ elegant

9. bleak : bare :: rustic : _____

   Ⓐ full   Ⓑ dignified   . dirty   Ⓓ simple

10. heavily decorated : ornate :: extravagant : _____

    Ⓐ brittle   Ⓑ lavish   Ⓒ brisk   Ⓓ hopeful

11. splurge : extravagant :: rampage : _____

    Ⓐ generous   . satisfying   Ⓒ dirty   Ⓓ destructive

12. indistinct : obvious :: average : _____
    Ⓐ gullible   Ⓑ exceptional   Ⓒ impudent   Ⓓ intentional

Name _____ Lesson 23 Date _____
(Answer ID # 0272867)

Study the relationship between the first set of words. Pick the word that completes the second pair with this same relationship.

1. hide : conceal :: disappear : _____

   Ⓐ bandit Ⓑ suspect Ⓒ hide Ⓓ vanish

2. complaint : _____ :: disability : handicap
   Ⓐ grievance Ⓑ principle Ⓒ altercation Ⓓ archive

3. unsure : absolute :: mild : _____

   Ⓐ scarce Ⓑ extreme Ⓒ easy Ⓓ negative

4. a penalty given to someone for doing wrong : punishment :: getting back at someone who has done something to hurt you : _____
   Ⓐ grievance Ⓑ penance Ⓒ munitions Ⓓ revenge

5. without giving up : relentlessly :: on purpose : _____

   Ⓐ vigorously Ⓑ deliberately Ⓒ mournfully Ⓓ grudgingly

6. a marketable good : commodity :: an illness : _____
   Ⓐ chattel Ⓑ malady Ⓒ branch Ⓓ adder

7. _____ : practical :: excessive : extravagant

   Ⓐ sensible Ⓑ bold Ⓒ showy Ⓓ urgent

8. extravagant : luxurious :: preposterous : _____

   Ⓐ absurd Ⓑ hidden Ⓒ scared Ⓓ unquestionable

9. careful : cautious :: purposeful : _____
   Ⓐ apprehensive Ⓑ deliberate Ⓒ luxurious Ⓓ oppressive

10. consign : entrust :: perambulate : _____

    Ⓐ forgive Ⓑ hide Ⓒ walk Ⓓ write

11. hidden : concealed :: pulled out : _____

    Ⓐ plucked Ⓑ fainted Ⓒ herded Ⓓ pushed

12. real : authentic :: intentional : _____
    Ⓐ plausible Ⓑ vigorous Ⓒ deliberate Ⓓ apprehensive

Name _____   Lesson 24   Date _____
                                                                                       (Answer ID # 0272867)

Study the relationship between the first set of words. Pick the word that completes the second pair with this same relationship.

1. abhor : _____ :: stun : shock

    (A) kiss   (B) scream   (C) hate   (D) sharing

2. a penalty given to someone for doing wrong : punishment :: getting back at someone who has done something to hurt you : _____

    (A) revenge   (B) munitions   (C) grievance   (D) penance

3. quick : slow :: kind : _____

    (A) merciless   (B) obstinate   (C) elegant   (D) unyielding

4. quick and light : nimble :: thick : _____

    (A) foul   (B) drastic   (C) dense   (D) crass

5. absurd : preposterous :: disbelieving : _____
    (A) relentless   (B) incredulous   (C) logical   (D) impudent

6. a marketable good : commodity :: an illness : _____

    (A) adder   (B) chattel   (C) branch   (D) malady

7. abundant : _____ :: drastic : extreme

    (A) loud   (B) uninhabited   . plentiful   (D) truthful

8. splurge : extravagant :: rampage : _____

    (A) satisfying   (B) destructive   (C) dirty   (D) generous

9. fetter : bind :: _____ : pretend
    (A) picket   (B) impart   (C) feign   (D) abate

10. _____ : practical :: excessive : extravagant

    (A) urgent   (B) . sensible   (C) . bold   (D) showy

11. _____ : ominous :: purposeful : deliberate

    (A) threatening   (B) sad   (C) truthful   (D) serene

12. _____ : persuade :: pretend : imagine

    (A) forgive   (B) hide   (C) leave   (D) . convince

100

Name _____ Lesson 25 Date _____
(Answer ID # 0200817)

Study the relationship between the first set of words. Pick the word that completes the second pair with this same relationship.

1. disinterest : boredom :: contentment : _____

   (A) anger   (B) relief   (C) resentment   (D) happiness

2. _____ : against the law :: illiterate : cannot read

   (A) secretive   (B) charitable   (C) illegal   (D) lawful

3. boisterous : _____ :: sympathetic : understanding

   (A) silent   (B) tight   (C) serious   (D) loud

4. tiredness : _____ :: daydreaming : reverie

   (A) precaution   (B) solace   (C) fatigue   (D) monotony

5. diligent : hardworking :: clever : _____

   (A) lever   (B) nice   (C) brainless   (D) smart

6. abrupt : sudden :: broad : _____

   (A) narrow   (B) wide   (C) odd   (D) slow

7. intense emotion : fervor :: boredom : _____

   (A) tedium   (B) chivalry   (C) scourge   (D) prestige

8. ending : interminable :: barren : _____

   (A) fertile   (B) permitted   (C) nimble   (D) discriminate

9. achievement : accomplishment :: praise : _____
   (A) opponent   (B) accolades   (C) criticism   (D) reverence

10. conciliating : soothing :: imperious : _____
    (A) bossy   (B) irritating   (C) helpful   (D) frightening

11. happy : sad :: excited : _____

    (A) disappointed (B) shocked   (C) disgusted   (D) confused

12. frantic : frenzied :: elated : _____

    (A) relaxed   (B) overjoyed   (C) surprised   (D) disgusted

Name _____   Lesson 26   Date _____
(- Answer ID # 0200817)

Study the relationship between the first set of words. Pick the word that completes the second pair with this same relationship.

1. hysteria : panic :: epidemic : _____

    (A) depredation   (B) stampede   (C) rogue   (D) plague

2. purchased : bought :: attempted : _____

    (A) tried   (B) used   (C) sold   (D) . proven

3. _____ : tired :: meek : shy
    (A) daunted   (B) scanty   (C) weary   (D) thwarted

4. obstreperous : unruly :: adroit : _____

    (A) skillful   (B) curious   (C) generous   (D) humane

5. animosity : hostility :: trepidation : _____

    (A) fear   (B) confidence   (C) hope   (D) bravery

6. disappear : vanish :: fear : _____

    (A) evaporate   (B) bravery   (C) terrify   (D) emerge

7. canny : careful :: frank : _____

    . trusting   (B) honest   (C) bold   (D) . generous

8. tiredness : _____ :: daydreaming : reverie

    (A) monotony   (B) solace   (C) precaution   (D) fatigue

9. _____ : doubtful :: demure : modest
    (A) gruff   (B) languid   (C) dubious   (D) malevolent

10. happy : sad :: excited : _____

    (A) disgusted   (B) confused   (C) shocked   (D) disappointed

11. soothe : calm :: elongate : _____

    (A) aggravate   (B) shorten   (C) lengthen   (D) honor

12. enthusiastic : ardent :: skillful : _____

    (A) . barbarous   (B) dexterous   (C) solitary   (D) fervid

Name _____   Lesson 27   Date _____
(Answer ID # 0200817)

Study the relationship between the first set of words. Pick the word that completes the second pair with this same relationship.

1. patriotism : pride :: terrorism : _____

    A hope   B retaliation   C fear   D indifference

2. calm : panicky :: relaxed : _____

    A tense   B elegant   C swift   D insufficient

3. ordinary : special :: humble : _____

    A shallow   B vain   C keen   D distressed

4. search : look for :: _____ : find

    A discover   B extinct   C mystery   D dinosaurs

5. hysteria : panic :: epidemic : _____

    A rogue   B stampede   C plague   D depredation

6. an expression of approval or honor : praise :: an admission of wrongdoings : _____
    A commitment   B ecology   C confession   D impression

7. tumultuous : disorderly :: _____ : horrible

    A brave   B frightening   C humbling   D gruesome

8. chintzy : stingy :: skeptical : _____

    A stubborn   B doubtful   C helpful   D strong

9. perfunctory : unconcerned :: wayward : _____

    A unruly   B meddling   C reluctant   D clumsy

10. find : discover :: uncover : _____

    A endure   B retract   C excavate   D fossil

11. happy : sad :: calm : _____

    A sleepy   B funny   C still   D panic

12. diminutive : gigantic :: defiant : _____

    A feeble   B obedient   C tremulous   D willful

Name _____   Lesson 28   Date _____
(Answer ID # 0289106)

Study the relationship between the first set of words. Pick the word that completes the second pair with this same relationship.

1. deceive : mislead :: decipher : _____

    A announce   **B** analyze   **C** solve   **D** confuse

2. the variation of a language in a particular region : dialect :: a group of stars forming a shape in the sky : _____

    A pinnacle   **B** plume   **C** constellation   **D** corridor

3. not enough rain : drought :: too much rain : _____

    A flood   **B** infestation   **C** famine   **D** fertile

4. drastic : moderate :: ancient : _____

    A juvenile   **B** artifact   **C** history   **D** extreme

5. rude : insolent :: capable : _____

    A dejected   **B** hardy   **C** competent   **D** epic

6. to set on fire : ignite :: to empty : _____

    A conform   **B** invigorate   **C** gorge   **D** vacate

7. joyful : happy :: celebrate : _____

    A mourn   **B** honor   **C** sad   **D** contemplate

8. leave : depart :: settle : _____

    A travel   **B** colonize   **C** celebrate   **D** land

9. perplexed : confused :: jocund : _____

    A greedy   **B** angry   **C** old   **D** cheerful

10. lament : mourn :: cajole : _____

    A tease   **B** celebrate   **C** persuade   **D** teach

11. blaming someone else for your mistake : lying :: copying someone else's homework : _____

    A morals   **B** impolite   **C** greedy   . cheating

12. plume : pen :: _____ : paper

    A pencil   **B** parchment   **C** brocade   **D** diagram

Name _____   Lesson 29   Date _____
(- Answer ID # 0289106)

Study the relationship between the first set of words. Pick the word that completes the second pair with this same relationship.

1. build : construct :: sell : _____

   Ⓐ price   Ⓑ design   Ⓒ market   Ⓓ distribute

2. light : heavy :: weak : _____
   Ⓐ change   Ⓑ endanger   Ⓒ strong   Ⓓ dull

3. plume : feather :: talon : _____

   Ⓐ eye   Ⓑ wing   Ⓒ beak   Ⓓ claw

4. leave : depart :: settle : _____
   . travel   Ⓑ colonize   Ⓒ celebrate   Ⓓ land

5. lament : mourn :: cajole : _____

   Ⓐ tease   Ⓑ celebrate   Ⓒ teach   Ⓓ persuade

6. to estimate incorrectly : miscalculate :: to adjust to new conditions : _____

   Ⓐ adapt   Ⓑ justify   Ⓒ navigate   Ⓓ avenge

7. _____ : generous :: cold-hearted : empathetic

   Ⓐ pleased   Ⓑ piteous   Ⓒ greedy   Ⓓ astonishing

8. amplify : intensify :: differentiate : _____

   Ⓐ encourage   Ⓑ adapt   Ⓒ distinguish   Ⓓ lead

9. replenish : _____ :: squelch : crush

   Ⓐ discuss   Ⓑ refill   Ⓒ regret   Ⓓ lurk

10. guess : speculate :: look forward to : _____
    Ⓐ exhilarate   Ⓑ apprehend   . anticipate   Ⓓ review

11. something that happened previously : preceding :: something that will happen soon : _____
    Ⓐ impending   Ⓑ coinciding   Ⓒ postponed   Ⓓ subsiding

12. torment : disturb :: replenish : _____

    Ⓐ discuss   Ⓑ regret   Ⓒ refill   Ⓓ lurk

Name _____   Lesson 30   Date _____

(Answer ID # 0289106)

Study the relationship between the first set of words. Pick the word that completes the second pair with this same relationship.

1. sorrowful : sad :: complicated : _____

   (A) intensive   (B) complete   (C) blunt   (D) complex

2. erratic : unpredictable :: nonchalant : _____

   (A) rippled   (B) casual   (C) indistinct   (D) dense

3. build : construct :: sell : _____

   (A) market   (B) distribute   (C) price   (D) design

4. unemotional : impassive :: hopeful : _____

   (A) presumptuous   (B) sarcastic   (C) optimistic   (D) hospitable

5. parasol : umbrella :: confection : _____

   (A) announcement   (B) sword   (C) competition   (D) candy

6. magazine : issue :: television program : _____

   (A) record   (B) episode   (C) movie   (D) page

7. majestic : regal :: complex : _____

   (A) intricate   (B) delicate   (C) derivative   (D) simple

8. poor soil where nothing can grow : barren :: rich soil that is good for farming : _____

   (A) nimble   (B) discriminate   (C) sparse   (D) fertile

9. drastic : moderate :: ancient : _____

   (A) extreme   (B) juvenile   (C) history   (D) artifact

10. articulate : eloquent :: intricate : _____

    (A) complex   (B) smooth   (C) delicate   (D) simple

11. sumac : plant :: calico : _____

    (A) fabric   (B) rafters   (C) food   (D) ravine

12. fierce : timid :: greedy : _____

    (A) hopeful   (B) jealous   (C) charitable   (D) sympathetic

Name _____   Lesson 31   Date _____
(Answer ID # 0944077)

Study the relationship between the first set of words. Pick the word that completes the second pair with this same relationship.

1. gleeful : _____ :: dismayed : disappointed

    (A) shy   (B) furious   (C) happy   (D) confused

2. naive : gullible :: uppity : _____
    (A) shrewd   (B) rational   (C) disoriented   (D) presumptuous

3. negative : electrons :: positive : _____

    (A) cells   (B) protons   (C) atoms   (D) neutrons

4. to calm : placate :: to spread out : _____
    (A) provoke   (B) careen   (C) disperse   (D) subside

5. quick : slow :: kind : _____

    (A) obstinate   (B) unyielding   (C) merciless   (D) elegant

6. peak : mountain :: _____ : house
    (A) roof   (B) fire   (C) floor   (D) door

7. debatable : controversial :: unopposed : _____
    (A) inclusive   (B) sarcastic   (C) metropolitan (D) unanimous

8. disturb : perturb :: fascinate : _____

    (A) subside   (B) intrigue   (C) decipher   (D) muster

9. mooring : securing :: meddling : _____

    (A) sheltering   (B) endangering   (C) dividing   (D) interfering

10. an illusion : hallucination :: a wide view : _____
    (A) panorama   (B) horizon   (C) multimedia   (D) peak

11. mournful : _____ :: obstinate : stubborn

    (A) coached   (B) haunted   (C) sorrowful   (D) honorable

12. a guess : speculation :: a goal : _____

    (A) admonition   (B) devotion   (C) fate   (D) aspiration

Name _____   Lesson 32   Date _____
(Answer ID # 0944077)

Study the relationship between the first set of words. Pick the word that completes the second pair with this same relationship.

1. curious : interested in how things work :: persevere : _____

   Ⓐ does not give up   Ⓑ refuses to change   Ⓒ scatterbrained   Ⓓ smart

2. revive : renew :: thrive : _____
   Ⓐ control   Ⓑ replenish   Ⓒ accept   Ⓓ prosper

3. to move clumsily : lumber :: to attack : _____

   Ⓐ subside   Ⓑ clamor   Ⓒ assail   Ⓓ resent

4. unsure : absolute :: mild : _____
   Ⓐ negative   Ⓑ cold   Ⓒ easy   Ⓓ extreme

5. a small stream : creek :: a range of hills or mountains : _____

   Ⓐ bank   Ⓑ ridge   Ⓒ breech   Ⓓ peak

6. sentimental : emotional :: optimistic : _____
   Ⓐ hopeful   Ⓑ humorous   Ⓒ negative   Ⓓ ridiculous

7. guess : speculate :: look forward to : _____

   Ⓐ cremate   Ⓑ exhilarate   Ⓒ distribute   Ⓓ anticipate

8. excited by frustration or nervousness : frantic :: careful : _____

   Ⓐ alert   Ⓑ cautious   . far away   Ⓓ unknown

9. worsen : improve :: disappoint : _____
   Ⓐ impress   Ⓑ petition   Ⓒ yearn   Ⓓ relinquish

10. careful : cautious :: purposeful : _____

    Ⓐ oppressive   Ⓑ deliberate   Ⓒ luxurious   Ⓓ apprehensive

11. recognize : identify :: subside : _____

    Ⓐ lengthen   Ⓑ disappear   Ⓒ diminish   Ⓓ hide

12. to calm : placate :: to spread out : _____

    Ⓐ disperse   Ⓑ provoke   Ⓒ careen   Ⓓ subside

Name _____ Lesson 33 Date _____

(Answer ID # 0944077)

Study the relationship between the first set of words. Pick the word that completes the second pair with this same relationship.

1. diminish : subside :: twist together : _____

   (A) imbue   (B) conquer   (C) entwine   (D) relent

2. peer : look :: spurn : _____
   (A) reject   (B) hide   (C) warn   . purchase

3. falter : advance :: abandon : _____

   (A) hope   (B) forward   (C) lose   (D) rescue

4. to fear greatly : _____ :: to look forward to : anticipate

   (A) dread   (B) evaporate   (C) perceive   (D) apprehend

5. funny : hilarious :: pitiful : _____

   (A) gullible   (B) generic   (C) pathetic   (D) disproportionate

6. peak : mountain :: _____ : house
   (A) floor   (B) fire   (C) roof   (D) door

7. to strive toward a goal : aspire :: to work together : _____

   (A) transfix   (B) resume   (C) embark   (D) collaborate

8. Relax : unwind :: Labor : _____

   (A) retire   (B) work   (C) job   (D) employ

9. stubborn : obstinate :: unashamed : _____
   (A) deprived   (B) inoculated   (C) antebellum   (D) unabashed

10. genuine : phony :: fragile : _____

    (A) unbearable   (B) amphibious   (C) inside   (D) indestructible

11. flourish : wave :: perspire : _____

    (A) reach   (B) sweat   (C) cut   (D) speak

12. to move clumsily : lumber :: to attack : _____

    (A) subside   (B) clamor   (C) assail   (D) resent

ANSWER KEYS

UNIT 2

boredom 1. Patrick started to play in his desk because of (**understanding, discovered, boredom**).

disputed 2. She (**claimed, disputed, illegally**) her claim to royalty.

ease 3. He adapted to his new surroundings with minimal (**weakly, disbelieving, ease**).

illegally 4. If you park (**illegally, nimble, disbelieving**), the police will impound your car.

solitary 5. Earlier he spent 12 years in prison, much of it in (**sharp, solitary, disbelieving**) confinement.

weakly 6. She become very (**claimed, weakly, alone**) when she was sick.

elegant 7. She looked like an (**weariness, elegant, abruptness**) princess in her new dress.

forgive 8. When you don't (**pacify, soothe, forgive**) someone, you feel bad.

pacify 9. We tried to (**doubtful, agile, pacify**) the baby's crying but only her mother could calm her down.

feebly 10. (**Feebly, Forgive, Disbelieving**) the old man walked to the store for food.

disgust 11. My mother looked at my messy bedroom and gave a groan of (**forgive, anxious, disgust**).

doubtful 12. I am (**feared, doubtful, boredom**) we will have practice today since it is raining.

weariness 13. A feeling of (**weariness, disputed, feared**) came over us at the end of the mile run in P.E. class.

affection 14. Mr. Bonna sent a Valentine to his wonderful wife to show his (**affection, abruptness, boredom**).

reluctance 15. His (**reluctance, discovered, abruptness**) to get on the plane was due to his fear of heights.

realistic 16. The painting is very (**discovered, realistic, anxious**).

disorderly 17. Why is this place so (**unruly, disorderly, weakly**)?

anxious 18. Cameron is (**anxious, nicely, abruptness**) for his sister to have a baby so he can be an uncle.

honest 19. Please give your (**honest, disgust, eagerness**) and open opinion on the questionnaire.

alone 20. It is not safe to go into the jungle (**alone, clearly, feebly**).

feared 21. When Alex brought home his report card, he greatly (**feared, suddenness, doubtful**) his parent's discipline.

agile 22. The athlete is (**weakly, playful, agile**) and quick.

clearly 23. I didn't hear (**ease, disagreement, clearly**) so I asked him to repeat the sentence.

praise 24. Sometimes faint (**boredom, fatigue, praise**) is worse than no praise at all.

understanding 25. Cognition means learning and (**understanding, feared, eagerness**) something.

dejected 26. The friends of the deceased man felt very melancholy and (**sharp, playful,**).

abruptness 27. The music stopped (**clearly, agile, abruptly**)

keen 28. He has a very (**keen, unruly, affection**) sense of humor.

panic 29. The loud noise caused Petra to (**panic, distasteful, boredom**).

sharp 30. Hawks have (**sharp, understanding, indifference**) talons.

playful 31. Joshua was in a very (**playful, distasteful, disgust**) mood.

proved 32. The illness (**indifference, feebly, proved**) to be very infectious since so many became sick.

eagerness 33. Katherine has played well in recent weeks, and her (**dejection, eagerness, indifference**) was evident at her piano recital.

disagreement 34. It will do no good to wrestle over this (**clearly, affection, disagreement**).

homely 35. Abraham Lincoln was often described as a (**elegant, reluctance, homely**) man in many ways.

disbelieving 36. His excuse for not doing his homework was (**agile, fatigue, disbelieving**) to his teacher.

discovered 37. I (**discovered, keen, sharp**) that ants are very smart little bugs.

unwillingness 38. Akua's bad temper and (**unwillingness, praise, disagreement**) to compromise caused him to be alienated from his peers.

admire 39. During fall, I like to walk through the park and (**suddenness, admire, eagerness**) the colorful leaves.

indifference 40. Adu showed (**disagreement, unwillingness, indifference**) when it came to watching boxing.

soothe 41. She gently talked to the injured pup trying to (**soothe, reluctance, praise**) its fear.

nimble 42. All athletes must be (**alone, nimble, discovered**) in order to compete.

insight 43. John seemed almost like a prophet with his (**insight, extent, claimed**).

unruly 44. The (**forgive, unruly, discovered**) children were not allowed recess time.

claimed 45. They (**claimed, honest, playful**) they did not despoil the store, but they were caught on video camera.

distasteful 46. That remark was crude and (**distasteful, solitary, agile**)!

fatigue 47. Doing the same thing over and over is tedious, causing mental (**indifference, fatigue, homely**).

Lesson 2 Answer Key 1037556			
detrimental	celebrate	fertile	dense
optimistic	pinnacle	greedy	blunt
replenish	drenched	excite	adapt
construct	presume	lofty	core

drenched 1. The rain ____ the people waiting for the bus.
detrimental 2. Using drugs is ____ to your health.
optimistic 3. She is ____ about her success in school.
blunt 4. My uncle gave me some ____ advice.
presume 5. Don't ____ that you know everything about a person even if they are your friend.
replenish 6. I will have to ____ the candy dish if you keep eating the chocolate.
core 7. The mantle of the earth is next to the ____.
greedy 8. Don't be ____ and eat all the cookies.
fertile 9. The flowers will thrive in the ____ soil.
excite 10. Do not ____ the dog because he might bite you.
pinnacle 11. The ____ of the tower was in need of repair..
celebrate 12. Memorial Day is an annual holiday that we ____ in May.
dense 13. The smog in Louisville is very ____.
adapt 14. I know you will ____ to your new surrounding quickly.
construct 15. Scientists use fossil records to ____ a geologic time scale.
lofty 16. The teacher has ____ goals for her students.

sentimental	insolent	similar	concise	revere
anticipate	endeavor	haughty	complex	
postponed	endanger	extreme	analyze	
exemplify	elevated	episode	torrid	

episode 17. The last ____ of the story made me cry.
sentimental 18. I am a very ____ person and I cherish the items from my grandmother.
revere 19. We ____ Jesus as the almighty power.
analyze 20. It is not always easy to ____ what went wrong.
concise 21. Be ____ when you are writing your report.
elevated 22. She has been ____ to manager.
endanger 23. The pollution will ____ the crops.
complex 24. That is a ____ math problem.
endeavor 25. I only ask that you always ____ to do your best.
similar 26. Purple and violet are ____ colors.
anticipate 27. Do you ____ what time the meeting will end?
insolent 28. The boy behaved like an ____ child.
haughty 29. Her ____ attitude did not make her a very popular girl.
extreme 30. He was in ____ pain.
torrid 31. Billy infatuations with Sally lead to a ____ affair.
exemplify 32. Soldier's fighting in Iraq ____ mettlesome behavior.
postponed 33. The doctor had ____ all the visits that were not pressing.

announcement	intricate	suppose	ravine	omit
suspicious	departure	conform	formal	
responsive	indicate	thrive	barren	
conclusion	incident	repeal	plume	

barren 34. The doctor told my aunt that she was ____.

formal 35. David rented a tuxedo to wear to the ____ dance.

repeal 36. I decided to ____ my offer to work on Saturday.

omit 37. I must remember to ____ my error on the final draft.

suppose 38. I ____ that I'll be finished with my homework soon.

conclusion 39. The author will astound her readers with the ____ of the book.

indicate 40. Please ____ on the map where we are.

ravine 41. They found some smooth rocks in the ____.

departure 42. Please affirm the ____ time.

suspicious 43. The police were looking for a ____ character.

announcement 44. The ____ was greeted with happiness.

plume 45. The lady had a large ____ in her hat.

responsive 46. The ____ audience clapped after the exciting show.

intricate 47. We could see many details in the ____ painting.

incident 48. The sad ____ was still very vivid in his memory.

thrive 49. Savanna grasses ____ in tropical climates.

conform 50. The new student tried to ____ to the rules of the new school.

Lesson 3
Answer Key 0770839

inundated 1. The students were (**inundated**, gullible, protective) with tons of homework for the holidays.

quantitative 2. "The glass holds .35 liters" is a (dissect, **quantitative**, thwarted) statement.

thwarted 3. The war (retire, **thwarted**, certify) peace in the country.

dissect 4. At times it can be difficult to (**dissect**, endanger, resume) a sentence into parts of speech.

migrate 5. Every year, millions of monarch butterflies (verbal, inundated, **migrate**) south to wintering grounds in Mexico.

intended 6. She (**intended**, thriving, exemplify) to go to the mall after school but went home instead.

economize 7. I was forced to (cautious, fragile, **economize**) when I lost my job.

cautious 8. I advised them to be (resume, **cautious**, retire).

noncommittal 9. The (obstinate, **noncommittal**, negative) answer stalled the investigation of the theft.

resume 10. The hearing was scheduled to (migrate, disappoint, **resume**) next week.

prone 11. All officials are supposedly human and therefore (**prone**, characteristic, economize) to error.

supplement 12. Many people take a vitamin (**supplement**, peak, thwarted) to feel healthier.

thriving 13. The new baby is (**thriving**, permission, thwarted) quite well.

verbal 14. Good (**verbal**, acknowledge, flourish) skills are an important asset during a job interview.

exemplify 15. We should always try to (endanger, obstinate, **exemplify**) Jesus with our own actions.

aspiration 16. Dr. Marfo's (refusal, **aspiration**, permission) is to become the best internist in Charlotte.

peak 17. Tim climbed to the (supplement, **peak**, falter) of the mountain.

protective 18. A mother bear is very (**protective**, permission, intended) of her cubs.

obstinate 19. Our boss was an (dissect, **obstinate**, supplement) person.

persevere 20. She will (characteristic, **persevere**, economize) in learning to play the piano.

falter 21. The music began to (obstinate, **falter**, flourish) as the music box ran down.

flourish 22. Tomatoes will (thriving, **flourish**, thwarted) in a very sunny garden if they are given water.

acknowledge 23. It is important to (noncommittal, **acknowledge**, quantitative) the work of others.

certify 24. Could you please (controversial, exemplify, **certify**) that these grades are correct?

disappoint 25. Please don't (aspiration, dissect, **disappoint**) me by not doing your homework.

subside 26. The pain in my head would not (verbal, resume, **subside**).

reject 27. The Bible warns of eternal retribution for those who (falter, **reject**, quantitative) Christ.

negative 28. The word had a (controversial, prone, **negative**) connotation.

characteristic 29. Honesty is a good (**characteristic**, aspiration, reject).

refusal 30. Her (**refusal**, reject, cautious) to sign the papers foregoes any acceptance of guilt of the crime.

retire 31. I usually (acknowledge, thriving, **retire**) to bed at nine o'clock.

endanger 32. The pollution will (**endanger**, anticipate, exemplify) the crops.

fragile 33. Mary's emotions are very (permission, falter, **fragile**) right now, and she cries easily.

anticipate 34. I (**anticipate**, supplement, exemplify) passing eighth-grade this time.

controversial 35. The referee's decision was very (**controversial**, quantitative, negative).

gullible 36. Being (**quantitative, gullible, acknowledge**), the young boy easily believed every word I said.

permission 37. Charlie asked his guardian for (**protective, permission, migrate**) to spend the night at my house.

Lesson 4 Answer Key 0586649

react 1. The class did not (**conceal, react, rustic**) badly to the surprise quiz.

govern 2. The king had a new realm to (**legitimate, govern, conceal**).

drastic 3. The President resorted to (**occupations, hazards, drastic**) measures to curb inflation.

legitimate 4. He had a (**legitimate, detest, grievances**) argument.

detest 5. Many people (**detest, grievances, arbitrary**) spiders and snakes.

assent 6. When a President does not (**govern, assent, pretend**) to legislation, he may veto the bill.

petty 7. People who are (**mystify, petty, extreme**) like to gossip.

entrust 8. I would never (**entrust, commodities, assent**) my funds to anyone who is so slipshod in managing his own affairs.

rustic 9. The unpainted log cabin was (**rustic, entrust, ambidextrous**) in appearance.

extravagant 10. Her husband bought her an (**extravagant, bashful, rustic**) birthday gift.

logical 11. You need to give a (**petty, occupations, logical**) explanation for your answer.

conceal 12. The prisoner was caught trying to (**drastic, conceal, defensive**) a weapon in his shoe.

conceal 13. Some people go to great extremes to (**govern, legitimate, conceal**) health problems.

extravagant 14. I think it's (**logical, hectic, extravagant**) to spend $500 on video game.

flamboyant 15. The movie star lead a (**flamboyant, abhor, react**) lifestyle.

deliberate 16. The jury will need to (**deliberate, assent, extravagant**) for hours before giving a verdict in the criminal case.

extreme 17. He really likes (**detest, extreme, commodities**) sports.

occupations 18. Many (**detest, occupations, elegant**) require more training after high school.

intentional 19. Her actions were (**elegant, arbitrary, intentional**).

petty 20. Don't let (**bashful, petty, sinister**) little problems upset you.

extreme 21. The plane nearly crashed because of (**arbitrary, sinister, extreme**) turbulence.

ambidextrous 22. Ngozi is able to write with both hands. Ngozi is (**ambidextrous, hectic, intentional**).

legitimate 23. You better have a (**intentional, legitimate, entrust**) reason for missing school yesterday.

hazards 24. There are many road (**detest, hazards, arbitrary**) in a construction area.

hectic 25. The last few days at school were very (**hazards, abhor, hectic**).

deliberate 26. The dance involved a (**deliberate, elegant, logical**) exaggeration of his awkwardness.

abhor 27. Some people (**abhor, legitimate, ambidextrous**) green vegetables, especially spinach.

defensive 28. Bill was very (**defensive, occupations, react**) of his ideas.

arbitrary 29. Since we felt the ruling was (**entrust, petty, arbitrary**), we were loath to obey it.

pretend 30. He tried to (**govern, pretend, petty**) that he hadn't heard the insult.

rustic 31. My mom did not want to stay in such a (**extravagant, rustic, abhor**) cabin for vacation.

hectic 32. Tranquility is a rare quality in the (**flamboyant, hectic, drastic**) modern age.

ambidextrous 33. Being (**ambidextrous, occupations, extreme**), Patrick could throw right-handed and hit left-handed.

deliberate 34. The mean boy played a (**react, deliberate, bashful**) trick on the little girl.

govern 35. People who (**pretend, extravagant, govern**) wickedly will not succeed.

pretend 36. We should never (**grievances, intentional, pretend**) to be someone that we are not.

assent 37. Those with courage will not (**flamboyant, assent, logical**) to actions they believe are wrong.

commodities 38. At the stock market people trade in (**commodities, deliberate, assent**)

react 39. All living things (**deliberate, hectic, react**) to change.

logical 40. Use your (**logical, extravagant, defensive**) reasoning to make a good decision.

intentional 41. It was done with (**bashful, conceal, intentional**) harm.

hazards 42. Our instructor directed us into a room where we would simulate our response to potential driving (**entrust, flamboyant, hazards**).

mystify 43. I am about to (**mystify, elegant, drastic**) you with my tricks!

conceal 44. Celebrities used to go to great extremes to (**conceal, drastic, sinister**) health problems.

flamboyant 45. Her costume was a (**pretend, conceal, flamboyant**) yellow.

govern 46. You must (**defensive, sinister, govern**) your class better.

flamboyant 47. The (**sinister, logical, flamboyant**) supermodel was stuck up.

arbitrary 48. The captain chose his team in an (**grievances, arbitrary, rustic**) manner.

sinister 49. The prison camp was a very (**sinister, mystify, elegant**) place.

grievances 50. The students filed a list of (**defensive, rustic, grievances**) because they felt mistreated.

abhor 51. I (**deliberate, mystify, abhor**) laziness in anyone!

legitimate 52. The contract on our house was (**abhor, ambidextrous, legitimate**).

occupations 53. He had many (**occupations, commodities, intentional**) to keep him busy.

bashful 54. When I feel (**bashful, petty, mystify**) I usually blush.

pretend 55. Lets (**pretend, entrust, flamboyant**) we are a prince and a princess.

elegant 56. Candles will be the perfect complement for an (**elegant, mystify, extreme**) dinner.

elegant 57. She looked like an (**react, elegant, rustic**) princess in her new dress.

sinister 58. The dark cave gave me a (**legitimate, sinister, drastic**) feeling.

drastic 59. These (**commodities, assent, drastic**) measures are necessary for your success in your final exams..

defensive 60. I exceeded the speed limit, so I got a ticket and had to take (**defensive, logical, hazards**) driving.

mystify 61. Her amazing story will (**mystify, grievances, deliberate**) you.

grievances 62. Instead of arguing, the students discussed their (**arbitrary, grievances, deliberate**).

entrust 63. I will (**extreme, ambidextrous, entrust**) this money to you for safekeeping.

drastic 64. Changing your hair color is very (**drastic, detest, extravagant**)!

detest 65. I (**detest, occupations, flamboyant**) the alarm clock when it beeps at 6 o'clock every morning.

UNIT 3

Lesson 5
Answer Key 0110077

1 affection
2 extent
3 abruptness
4 elegant
5 agile
6 unwillingness
7 disagreement
8 boredom
9 reluctance
10 alone
11 fatigue
12 unruly
13 feared
14 ease
15 anxious
16 panic
17 dejection
18 pacify
19 nimble
20 feebly
21 doubtful
22 illegally
23 distasteful

24 soothe
25 forgive
26 homely
27 honest
28 indifference
29 clearly
30 proved
31 admire
32 playful
33 realistic
34 insight
35 suddenness
36 disbelieving
37 disorderly
38 weariness
39 nicely
40 solitary
41 claimed
42 understanding
43 praise
44 sharp
45 disgust
46 discovered

47 disputed
48 keen
49 eagerness
50 weakly

Lesson 6
Answer Key 0645928

1 plume
2 elevated
3 optimistic
4 thrive
5 indicate
6 incident
7 concise
8 celebrate
9 revere
10 departure
11 endeavor
12 excite
13 insolent
14 endanger
15 greedy
16 core

17 drenched
18 lofty
19 presume
20 repeal
21 similar
22 formal
23 barren
24 announcement
25 conclusion
26 responsive
27 exemplify
28 pinnacle
29 omit
30 torrid
31 detrimental
32 fertile
33 postponed
34 construct
35 episode
36 anticipate
37 suppose
38 adapt
39 intricate
40 extreme

Lesson 6 Answer Key 0645928 Continued	Lesson 7 Answer Key 0142833	Lesson 8 Answer Key 0173406	
	1 intended	**1** deliberate	
41 dense	**2** thwarted	**2** rustic	
42 suspicious	**3** protective	**3** arbitrary	
43 blunt	**4** disappoint	**4** legitimate	
44 analyze	**5** flourish	**5** conceal	
45 sentimental	**6** falter	**6** flamboyant	
46 ravine	**7** noncommittal	**7** react	
47 complex	**8** peak	**8** assent	
48 replenish	**9** controversial	**9** sinister	
49 conform	**10** verbal	**10** defensive	
50 haughty	**11** retire	**11** extreme	
	12 economize	**12** bashful	
	13 characteristic	**13** commodities	
	14 prone	**14** detest	
	15 refusal	**15** govern	
	16 thriving	**16** hectic	
	17 certify	**17** grievances	
	18 exemplify	**18** abhor	
	19 persevere	**19** mystify	
	20 inundated	**20** ambidextrous	
	21 cautious	**21** entrust	
	22 quantitative	**22** logical	
	23 supplement	**23** elegant	
	24 resume	**24** extravagant	
	25 acknowledge	**25** occupations	
	26 aspiration	**26** drastic	
	27 fragile	**27** hazards	
	28 obstinate	**28** petty	
	29 endanger	**29** pretend	
	30 permission	**30** intentional	
	31 gullible		
	32 anticipate		
	33 migrate		
	34 dissect		
	35 reject		
	36 subside		
	37 negative		

UNIT 4

Lesson 9
Answer Key 1083504

1. **disorderly**
   (A) Not good-looking. Plain and simple.
   (B) having or showing an inclination to face facts and deal with them sensibly
   ● Not in order, not disciplined

2. **nimble**
   (A) Find unexpectedly.
   ● Moving quickly and lightly.
   (C) Apathy demonstrated by an absence of emotional reactions.

3. **illegally**
   (A) The opposite of awkward; graceful
   ● Not acceptable, lawful or within the law
   (C) A feeling of horrified distaste for something

4. **distasteful**
   (A) Mentally quick.
   ● Unpleasant, disagreeable, objectionable or offensive
   (C) Afraid or nervous about what may happen

5. **fatigue**
   (A) A thin, fine edge or a pointed tip.
   (B) Open to debate.
   ● Great tiredness resulting from hard physical or mental work.

6. **playful**
   (A) To be exhausted - very tired
   (B) To show that something is true or correct.
   ● Full of play; fond of playing

7. **panic**
   ● An overwhelming feeling of fear and anxiety.
   (B) Appreciating the reasons for a mistake.
   (C) Characterized by quickness, lightness, and ease of movement; nimble. Mentally quick or alert: an agile mind.

8. **extent**
   ● The range, distance, or space over or through which something extends.
   (B) See for the first time; make a discovery.
   (C) Having or demonstrating ability to recognize or draw fine distinctions.

9. **understanding**
   ● knowing what something means or how it works
   (B) Of seemingly effortless beauty in form or proportion.
   (C) Reject as false; refuse to accept.

10. **disgust**
    ● A feeling of horrified distaste for something
    (B) The state of feeling tired, restless, and uninterested
    (C) A positive feeling of liking.

11. **proved**
    (A) Capable of being trusted, not stealing, cheating, or lying.
    (B) A feeling of uneasiness. To feel worried, nervous, or eager. You may feel this before a big math test.
    ● Established beyond doubt.

12. **affection**
    (A) Lack of understanding or unity
    (B) Using facts and good sense to evaluate people, things, or situations; concerned with the practical; resembling real life
    ● A feeling of kindness, fondness, love for someone or something

13. **claimed**
    ● To demand as yours or to state something strongly.
    (B) To make less worried, pained or troubled.
    (C) The quality of happening with headlong

14. **weariness**
    (A) The quality of happening with headlong haste or without warning.
    ● Worn out in strength, energy, or freshness
    (C) To argue; to quarrel.

haste or without warning. Sudden	

15. feared ● Be uneasy or apprehensive about. (B) Clear or deep perception of a situation. (C) The feeling of having nothing to do, a tedious state	**16. indifference** ● The trait of remaining calm and seeming not to care; a casual lack of concern. (B) Not attractive in appearance; plain. (C) Unwilling to submit to authority.
17. alone (A) Sharp and quick with the five senses; eager ● Without other persons or things. (C) To be unsure about something.	**18. dejection** (A) Excited, scared, don't know what to do. ● Lowness of spirits; sadness; depression (C) The power or act of seeing into a situation.
19. feebly ● Not having strength or sick; weak (B) Truly or really; in agreement with the truth, facts, or reality. (C) Impossible to discipline; refusing to obey	**20. forgive** (A) The state of not wanting to do something. ● Stop blaming somebody or stop feeling angry with somebody about something. (C) Open to suspicion.
21. ease (A) Having a thin cutting edge or fine point. (B) Lack of understanding or unity ● Freedom from constraint or embarrassment.	**22. boredom** (A) A feeling of kindness, fondness, love for someone or something ● The feeling of having nothing to do, a tedious state (C) A state of melancholy depression.
23. nicely (A) lack of enthusiasm: unwillingness or lack of enthusiasm ● good, pleasant, agreeable, pretty, kind, polite, etc., (C) Cause to be more favorably inclined; gain the good will of.	**24. sharp** (A) Lacking companions or companionship. ● Having a thin cutting edge or fine point. (C) To look up to someone or something with respect
25. anxious (A) Being real; common sense decisions (B) Refined or tastefully lavish, excellent, splendid. ● A feeling of uneasiness. To feel worried, nervous, or eager. You may feel this before a big math test.	**26. abruptness** ● The quality of happening with headlong haste or without warning. Sudden (B) To stop blaming or feeling anger toward someone; pardon or excuse. (C) Using facts and good sense to evaluate people, things, or situations; concerned with the practical; resembling real life
27. pacify (A) A quarrel; not able to come to an agreement; not of the same opinion ● Cause to be more favorably inclined; gain the good will of. (C) To quiet or calm someone	**28. elegant** ● Refined or tastefully lavish, excellent, splendid. (B) When you are by your self (C) The ability to perceive the true nature of something.
29. eagerness	**30. disagreement**

(A) Not following rules; hard to manage	(A) Unattractive, plain, simple, ordinary.
(B) Quick in thinking and understanding.	● Lack of understanding or unity
● A strong desire to do something.	(C) Strong feelings of dislike.

31. reluctance
- (A) To please by praise or attention.
- ● The state of not wanting to do something.
- (C) Intense or sharp.

32. admire
- (A) To be by yourself.
- (B) Argued; disagreed; fought over
- ● To look up to someone or something with respect

33. honest
- ● True to yourself and others.
- (B) Move gently or carefully.
- (C) Unreasonable fear causing someone to lose control

34. homely
- ● Not attractive in appearance; plain.
- (B) To honor with words or song.
- (C) Something beautiful, suggesting great wealth.

35. soothe
- (A) To say something good about something
- (B) Look up to with appreciation.
- ● Give moral or emotional strength to.

36. unwillingness
- (A) To say that something belongs to you
- (B) Not pleasing in odor or taste.
- ● Not wanting to do something

37. keen
- (A) To make peaceful or calm; to soothe
- ● Having or demonstrating ability to recognize or draw fine distinctions.
- (C) To find, see, or learn something, usually for the first time

38. solitary
- ● Without the company of others. Single, lone. Far away from society.
- (B) A tired felling that lowers your level of activity.
- (C) Lacking physical strength or vitality.

39. insight
- (A) A positive feeling of wanting to push ahead with something.
- ● Clear or deep perception of a situation.
- (C) Clean and free from anything that makes it hard to see.

40. doubtful
- (A) Cause to be more favorably inclined; gain the good will of.
- ● Open to suspicion.
- (C) To find, see, or learn something, usually for the first time

41. realistic
- - Being real; common sense decisions
- (B) The trait of remaining calm and seeming not to care; a casual lack of concern.
- (C) Impossible to discipline; refusing to obey

42. weakly
- (A) Find unexpectedly.
- ● Lacking physical strength or vitality.
- (C) A feeling of kindness, fondness, love for someone or something

43. praise
- ● To say something good about something
- (B) The range, distance, or space over or through which something extends.
- (C) Not following rules; hard to manage

44. unruly
- ● Unwilling to submit to authority.
- (B) Not having strength or sick; weak
- (C) The quality of happening with headlong haste or without warning. Sudden

45. suddenness

46. disputed

(A) To please by praise or attention.	(A) A don't care attitude.
● The quality of happening with headlong haste or without warning.	(B) Make easier.
(C) Unattractive, plain, simple, ordinary.	● Open to debate.

Lesson 10
Answer Key 0278320

1. episode	2. revere
● An occurrence that has happened during the course of a day.	(A) Adapt or conform oneself to new or different conditions.
(B) Grow stronger.	(B) To build something or create.
(C) Characterized by intense emotion.	● To honor, to highly respect, to venerate, to regard with awe.

3. plume	4. anticipate
● A structure or form that is like a long feather:	● Realize beforehand.
(B) To show; to make known.	(B) Not able to produce growing plants or crops.
(C) Hard to pass through because of dense growth.	(C) To delete; an official or legal cancellation.

5. conform	6. omit
(A) Related in appearance or nature; alike though not the same.	(A) Containing many details or small parts that are skillfully made or assembled
(B) Closely crowded together.	● To leave out or unmentioned.
● Adapt or conform oneself to new or different conditions.	(C) This deepest layer is at the center of Earth.

7. endanger	8. concise
(A) To survive and do well.	● Say a lot with few words.
(B) Regard something as probable or likely.	(B) To follow an established pattern or standard
● To put in a dangerous situation; to threaten.	(C) A part of a broadcast serial.

9. insolent	10. presume
(A) To fill something again. To resupply.	● To assume, to believe something is true before you know whether or not it is.
(B) When something is very damaging to something else	(B) A formal printed notice, as of a wedding or other event
● Showing lack of respect to rank or authority.	(C) Rude or arrogant in conduct and speech

11. complex	12. similar
(A) A single distinct event.	(A) A happening that is distinctive in a series of related events.
(B) To assume, to believe something is true before you know whether or not it is.	● Related in appearance or nature; alike though not the same.
● Intricate, not simple, composed of two or more related parts	(C) Gain in wealth.

13. formal	14. sentimental

A. Expressed in a few words.

B. To adjust to a new situation or surrounding.

●. Very correct, following all the rules of conduct and/or dress

---

●. Something that appeals to the emotions or romantic feelings.

B. A sudden decline in strength or number or importance.

C. Anything that causes damage or injury.

---

15. **drenched**

A. To do something special or have festivities to observe an event or day.

B. An event that is unusual.

●. Soaked or very wet.

---

16. **blunt**

A. To believe to create an idea of something.

B. Anything that causes damage or injury.

●. Make less sharp.

---

17. **exemplify**

A. Realize beforehand.

●. To illustrate or to serve as an example or by example.

C. The innermost layer of Earth

---

18. **conclusion**

●. The end of a book, play, or movie.

B. Leave undone or leave out.

C. Of imposing height; especially standing out above others.

---

19. **elevated**

●. Raised to a higher level.

B. A day or holiday when people do something enjoyable.

C. That which causes one to suspect guilt or wrong-doing.

---

20. **construct**

A. Existing in the greatest possible degree.

●. To build something or create.

C. Burning hot; extremely and unpleasantly hot.

---

21. **detrimental**

A. To think or believe something is true.

B. Very high or very high moral value.

●. when something is very damaging to something else

---

22. **suspicious**

A. the hard center of an apple or pear

●. Likely to suspect or distrust.

C. Arrogant; vainly proud; showing disdain to those one views as unworthy.

---

23. **departure**

A. An official or legal cancellation.

●. To leave, especially to go on a journey.

C. Abrupt; frank; outspoken.

---

24. **core**

A. very thick or crowded in space.

B. Quick to react to something.

●. the hard center of an apple or pear

---

25. **suppose**

A. Bearing in abundance especially offspring.

●. To believe to create an idea of something.

Readily reacting to suggestions and influences.

---

26. **celebrate**

●. To do something special or have festivities to observe an event or day.

B. Able to produce more, especially land that is full of nutrients.

C. Having or displaying great dignity or nobility.

---

27. **responsive**

●. Susceptible to suggestion.

B. A sudden decline in strength or number or importance.

C. To leave undone or leave out.

---

28. **fertile**

A. Be excited or anxious about.

●. Able to produce more, especially land that is full of nutrients.

C. Proper and not casual.

29. **postponed**
   (A) Try hard; Make an effort; strive.
   (B) A brief section of a literary or dramatic work that forms part of a connected series.
   ● Put off to a later time.

30. **pinnacle**
   (A) Make a prediction about; tell in advance.
   ● (Architecture) a slender upright spire at the top of a buttress of tower.
   (C) Used of a knife or other blade; not sharp.

31. **incident**
   (A) Something that appeals to the emotions or romantic feelings.
   ● A single distinct event.
   (C) Accept without verification or proof.

32. **adapt**
   (A) Say a lot with few words.
   (B) A token of honor or achievement
   ● Changing to get used to something new.

33. **ravine**
   (A) Figuring out something by looking at its parts.
   (B) Far beyond what is usual in magnitude or degree.
   ● A narrow valley that is similar to a canyon or gorge.

34. **replenish**
   (A) To have parties or fun to enjoy a special day.
   (B) Existing in the greatest possible degree.
   ● Fill something that had previously been emptied.

35. **endeavor**
   (A) Marked by great fruitfulness.
   (B) Prevent from being included or considered or accepted.
   ● Try hard; Make an effort; strive.

36. **thrive**
   (A) To assume, to believe something is true before you know whether or not it is.
   ● Grow stronger.
   (C) A purposeful or industrious undertaking (especially one that requires effort or boldness).

37. **barren**
   (A) To do certain things because of a special occasion.
   ● Not able to produce growing plants or crops.
   (C) A lofty peak.

38. **torrid**
   (A) To illustrate or to serve as an example or by example.
   (B) Effusively or insincerely emotional.
   ● Burning hot; extremely and unpleasantly hot.

39. **announcement**
   (A) To think or believe something is true.
   (B) Make less sharp.
   ● A formal printed notice, as of a wedding or other event

40. **repeal**
   (A) Be excited or anxious about.
   (B) One of two ends or opposites
   ● To undo a law or tax

41. **lofty**
   (A) To leave undone or leave out.
   ● Of imposing height; especially standing out above others.
   (C) Complicated or tangled, highly involved.

42. **indicate**
   ● To show; to make known.
   (B) To behave or think like others
   (C) Very high or very high moral value.

43. **intricate**
   (A) Abrupt; frank; outspoken.
   (B) Related in appearance or nature; alike

44. **greedy**
   (A) Having or showing tender, sensitive feelings.

though not the same. ● Containing many details or small parts that are skillfully made or assembled	Ⓑ To study carefully in order to determine what something is, what its parts are, or how its parts fit together. ● Wanting to have more than you need
45. dense Ⓐ A single distinct event. ● Hard to pass through because of dense growth. Ⓒ The end of a book, play, or movie.	**46. optimistic** ● Hopeful that things will turn out in the best possible way. Ⓑ A narrow valley that is similar to a canyon or gorge. Ⓒ Done in a proper way. A formal letter or statement is stiff, rigid, proper, and perfect.
47. haughty ● Arrogant; vainly proud; showing disdain to those one views as unworthy. Ⓑ To study carefully in order to determine what something is, what its parts are, or how its parts fit together. Ⓒ Very correct, following all the rules of conduct and/or dress	**48. analyze** Ⓐ A purposeful or industrious undertaking (especially one that requires effort or boldness). ● To study carefully in order to determine what something is, what its parts are, or how its parts fit together. Ⓒ Rich soil that is good for growing crops.

Lesson 12
Answer Key 0773915

1. prone Ⓐ Begin again; take again; occupy again ● Lying face downward. Ⓒ To keep going even in tough times	**2. noncommittal** Ⓐ To give up one's job. ● Very reluctant to give out information. Ⓒ amount such as age, weight, or percent
3. disappoint Ⓐ Stubborn, especially in holding an attitude, opinion, or course of action ● To let someone down; to not make someone proud of satisfied Ⓒ Be excited or anxious about.	**4. quantitative** Ⓐ Something causing a disagreement, argument or a dispute. Ⓑ To move unsteadily or to hesitate in speaking. ● amount such as age, weight, or percent
5. thwarted ● To keep from doing or succeeding; foil Ⓑ Having a tendency (to); often used in combination. Ⓒ Movement of a group (people, animals or birds) from one place to another	**6. acknowledge** ● To let someone know that one has received something Ⓑ Realize beforehand. Ⓒ A summary, usually in chronological order, of your work experience.
7. inundated Ⓐ Difficult to manage, control, or subdue Ⓑ The highest point; top. ● Made powerless especially by too much of something	**8. migrate** Ⓐ causing a disagreement or debate ● Move from one country or region to another and settle there. Ⓒ Be persistent, refuse to stop.
9. negative	**10. refusal**

● A piece of photographic film showing an image with black and white tones reversed. Ⓑ Sink to a lower level or form a depression. Ⓒ Refers to amounts or numbers of things.	● To say you will not do or accept something. Ⓑ Put in a dangerous, disadvantageous, or difficult position. Ⓒ Remaining constant to a purpose; be persistent, refuse to stop.
11. anticipate Ⓐ To start or go on again after stopping. Ⓑ To say no to something or someone ● Be excited or anxious about.	**12. certify** Ⓐ To recognize the status or rights of ● officially verified Ⓒ To grow and succeed.
13. cautious Ⓐ Lacking solidity or strength. Ⓑ To take something apart to analyze it ● To be very careful and not take any chances	**14. retire** ● Pull back or move away or backward. Ⓑ Likely to have or do. Ⓒ To hesitate; the act of pausing uncertainly; be unsure or weak.
15. dissect Ⓐ To answer that a message was received. ● To take something apart to analyze it Ⓒ officially verified	**16. protective** Ⓐ Refuse to accept. ● Covering or shielding from injury. Ⓒ Clarify by giving an example of.
17. flourish ● To grow strong, to grow abundantly, to thrive or prosper. Ⓑ Guarantee as meeting a certain standard. Ⓒ Act in advance of; deal with ahead of time.	**18. falter** Ⓐ To confirm as true, accurate, or genuine, especially in writing. ● To move unsteadily or to hesitate in speaking. Ⓒ Of or relating to or formed from words in general.
19. gullible Ⓐ Expect questions, to look ahead at things that may happen ● Easily deceived, quick to believe Ⓒ Communicated in the form of words.	**20. endanger** ● Put in a dangerous, disadvantageous, or difficult position. Ⓑ Consent or approval to do something. Ⓒ Very reluctant to give out information.
21. economize Ⓐ Dismiss from consideration. Ⓑ A special quality or feature of something or someone. ● To save money; to be frugal	**22. controversial** Ⓐ Allowing someone to do something. Ⓑ Expressed in words; not written ● Something that causes arguing about differences of opinion.
23. obstinate Ⓐ To have bad or unpleasant feelings. ● Stubborn, especially in holding an attitude, opinion, or course of action Ⓒ Authorize officially.	**24. exemplify** Ⓐ To serve as a model or be a very good example of. Ⓑ Vulnerably delicate. Ⓒ A reply of denial.
25. fragile	**26. resume**

126

(A) Something that helps keep things or people from being damaged attacked, stolen, or injured.	● A summary, usually in chronological order, of your work experience.
● Delicate, easily broken or damaged	(B) Lying horizontal with the face down
(C) To have in mind as a purpose or goal	(C) Grow less; die down; become less active; abate

27. **thriving**	28. **subside**
(A) Withdraw from active participation.	(A) To refuse or accept, use, grant, or consider
● To flourish; to be successful in growth; to grow vigorously	● Sink to a lower level or form a depression.
(C) something that completes or makes an addition <dietary supplements>	(C) Unwilling to take a clear position

29. **permission**	30. **characteristic**
● Allowing someone to do something.	● A special or distinguishing quality.
(B) Expressed in spoken words.	(B) When someone says something is O.K.
(C) Cut open or cut apart.	(C) Wear off or die down.

31. **aspiration**	32. **reject**
(A) Go to bed in order to sleep.	(A) A special or distinguishing quality.
● A strong desire to do something	(B) Sink down or precipitate.
(C) To get smaller, lessen.	● Refuse to accept.

33. **persevere**	34. **verbal**
(A) To add to or bring to completion	(A) A showy gesture.
(B) Grow stronger. To flourish. Growing	(B) Overwhelmed; filled up with too much to handle.
● Be persistent, refuse to stop.	● Of or relating to or formed from words in general.

35. **peak**	36. **supplement**
(A) To hesitate; the act of pausing uncertainly; be unsure or weak.	● Something that completes or makes an addition <dietary supplements>
● The highest point; top.	(B) To move unsteadily or to hesitate in speaking.
(C) Communicated in the form of words.	(C) Allowing someone to do something.

Lesson 12
Answer Key 0632822

1. **react**	2. **defensive**
● Act in response to another action	● To be on guard against attack, be it verbal or physical
(B) To make someone responsible for something.	(B) Another word for a complaint.
(C) Synonyms: threatening, ominous, menacing, dire, disturbing, evil, harmful, fearful	(C) Anything that is bought or sold, though the term is most often used to refer to products made from natural resources
3. **ambidextrous**	4. **occupations**
● A person who is skilled at using both their right and left hands.	● Any activity that occupies a person's attention.
(B) Tasteful, stylish, and beautiful	(B) Mysteriously wicked, evil or dishonest
(C) When you dislike a thing or person very much.	(C) To do something on purpose (when you want to do something).
5. **mystify**	6. **extravagant**
(A) Shy, not at ease, especially in a social setting	● Recklessly wasteful.
(B) Merchandise which can be sold or traded	(B) Of seemingly effortless beauty in form or proportion.
● To confuse or puzzle someone.	(C) By conscious design or purpose.
7. **govern**	8. **flamboyant**
(A) complaints about the unfair practice of Parliament	● Very colorful, showy, or elaborate
● To lead by laws or rules.	(B) Someone who feels shy, especially around new people
(C) To dislike intensely, loathe, despise	(C) Carefully thought out; not hasty.
9. **extreme**	10. **abhor**
(A) Wasteful, especially with money.	● To dislike intensely, loathe, despise
● Farthest in any direction; very intense; radical (adj.)	(B) The principal activity in your life that you do to earn money.
(C) Lawful, rightful; reasonable, justifiable	(C) Existing in the greatest possible degree.
11. **deliberate**	12. **rustic**
(A) Based on chance rather than reason	(A) Able to write with both hands
(B) To agree or give approval.	● Characteristic of rural life.
● Carefully thought out; not hasty.	(C) Unrestrained in especially feelings.
13. **assent**	14. **petty**
● To agree or express agreement.	(A) Make legal.
(B) Dislike intensely; feel antipathy or aversion towards.	(B) Spending too much money, especially on luxuries.
(C) Discuss the pros and cons of an issue.	● Inferior in rank or status.

15. **commodities**
   - (A) Things that cause harm or danger
   - (B) Awkwardly simple and provincial.
   - ● Merchandise which can be sold or traded

16. **arbitrary**
   - (A) Very busy, excited or confusing
   - ● Based on chance rather than reason
   - (C) Mean, small-minded, selfish

17. **intentional**
   - (A) To hide or keep secret, to place out of sight
   - ● By conscious design or purpose.
   - (C) To dislike strongly; to hate

18. **legitimate**
   - (A) Merchandise which can be sold or traded
   - (B) To be in charge of; to control or rule.
   - ● Authorized, sanctioned by, or in accordance with law.

19. **detest**
   - (A) Make believe; make something up
   - ● To dislike strongly; to hate
   - (C) Prevent from being seen or discovered.

20. **sinister**
   - ● Mysteriously wicked, evil or dishonest
   - (B) Stylish; rich and fine in quality
   - (C) By conscious design or purpose.

21. **bashful**
   - (A) To be in charge of; to control or rule.
   - (B) Acting rapidly or violently; extreme in effect: severe
   - ● Someone who feels shy, especially around new people

22. **conceal**
   - (A) Orderly and with intelligence. Make sense.
   - ● To prevent from being seen or discovered
   - (C) To agree to something, especially after thoughtful consideration.

23. **grievances**
   - ● complaints about the unfair practice of Parliament
   - (B) Deciding just because you feel like it
   - (C) Contemptibly narrow in outlook.

24. **pretend**
   - (A) Stylish; rich and fine in quality
   - (B) Very busy, excited or confusing
   - ● To give a false show in order to trick or deceive.

25. **drastic**
   - (A) Synonyms: threatening, ominous, menacing, dire, disturbing, evil, harmful, fearful
   - ● Acting rapidly or violently; extreme in effect: severe
   - (C) To prevent from being seen or discovered

26. **hectic**
   - ● very busy, lots of things going on
   - (B) Authorized, sanctioned by, or in accordance with law.
   - (C) Marked by careful consideration or reflection.

27. **entrust**
   - ● To make someone responsible for something.
   - (B) Any activity that occupies a person's attention.
   - (C) Things that cause harm or danger

28. **elegant**
   - (A) To be on guard against attack, be it verbal or physical
   - ● Of seemingly effortless beauty in form or proportion.
   - (C) Forceful and extreme and rigorous.

29. **hazards**
   - (A) Marked by careful consideration or reflection.
   - (B) Anything that is bought or sold, though the term is most often used to refer to products made from natural resources

30. **logical**
   - (A) Mean, small-minded, selfish
   - (B) To hide or keep secret, to place out of sight
   - ● Orderly and with intelligence. Make sense.

⬭ Things that cause harm or danger	

UNIT 5

Lesson 13 Answer Key 0126014	Lesson 14 Answer Key 0867403		
1 agile	1 extravagant		
2 understanding	2 react		
3 disagreement	3 legitimate		
4 homely	4 pretend		
5 disorderly	5 extreme		
6 nimble	6 hectic		
7 honest	7 entrust		
8 fatigue	8 petty		
9 sharp	9 drastic		
10 elegant	10 deliberate		
11 admire	11 intentional		
12 disgust	12 arbitrary		
13 praise	13 rustic		
14 keen	14 bashful		
15 anxious	15 elegant		
16 affection	16 conceal		
17 alone	17 logical		
18 solitary	18 detest		
19 doubtful	19 abhor		
20 extent	20 sinister		

Lesson 15

Across:
6. ARBITRARY
7. DELIBERATE
8. PETTY
9. MYSTIFY
11. LEGITIMATE

Down:
1. PRETENENE
2. CONCEAL
3. DETEST
4. EXTREME
5. FLOOMAN
10. R
REENACT

UNIT 6

Word Search:

```
    Y L     E A S E                 E
      L U       W     E A G E R N E S S
    D   R F     E                 O
    I D   T  E Y       A         L
    S I   N   D A     R     A K
    P S E E     R L     I   E                   P
    U T C M         O P   E N       I     R
    T A N E         S N     E   N       O
    E S A E G N I V E I L E B S I D V T C
    D T T R             D   I   S E   N I
      E C G                 G   D     A N
      F U A                 H         G A
      U L S             T             E P
      L E I   S O L I T A R Y         L
        R D                 T S E N O H E
  P A C I F Y S H A R P
```

1 DISAGREEMENT
2 SHARP
3 RELUCTANCE
4 HONEST
5 DISORDERLY
6 PROVED
7 DISTASTEFUL
8 PANIC
9 DISPUTED
10 INSIGHT
11 WEARINESS
12 EASE
13 KEEN
14 EAGERNESS
15 PACIFY
16 ALONE

17 SOLITARY
18 DISBELIEVING
19 ELEGANT
20 PLAYFUL

Lesson 17 Answer Key 0654047		Lesson 18 Answer Key 1043575		Lesson 19 Answer Key 0800933		
1	d	1	b	1	e	
2	e	2	c	2	b	
3	b	3	c	3	c	
4	a	4	d	4	e	
5	d	5	e	5	d	
6	c	6	a	6	e	
7	d	7	b	7	c	
8	e	8	a	8	c	
9	b	9	e	9	b	
10	a	10	d	10	c	

UNIT 7

Lesson 20 Answer Key 1092820	Lesson 21 Answer Key 0193394		
1 prone	1 intentional		
2 inundated	2 flamboyant		
3 resume	3 logical		
4 quantitative	4 pretend		
5 acknowledge	5 legitimate		
6 protective	6 rustic		
7 subside	7 defensive		
8 endanger	8 petty		
9 fragile	9 drastic		
10 certify	10 elegant		
11 verbal	11 conceal		
12 negative	12 deliberate		
13 noncommittal	13 bashful		
14 flourish	14 hectic		
15 permission	15 react		
16 anticipate	16 assent		
17 peak	17 ambidextrous		
18 disappoint	18 govern		
19 controversial	19 extravagant		
20 reject	20 abhor		

UNIT 8

Lesson 22
Answer Key 0272867

1. conceal : _____ :: baffle : confuse

   Ⓐ appear   Ⓑ fire   ⬤ hide   Ⓓ review

2. sleep : doze :: awaken : _____

   Ⓐ mystify   ⬤ rouse   Ⓒ fluster   . wince

3. without giving up : relentlessly :: on purpose : _____

   Ⓐ mournfully   Ⓑ vigorously   Ⓒ grudgingly   ⬤ deliberately

4. quick and light : nimble :: thick : _____

   Ⓐ crass   Ⓑ foul   ⬤ dense   . drastic

5. commodities : products :: alternatives : _____

   Ⓐ promises   ⬤ options   Ⓒ requirements   Ⓓ strengths

6. elegant : graceful :: dainty : _____

   Ⓐ flexible   Ⓑ soft   ⬤ delicate   Ⓓ decorated

7. naturally, without thought : instinctively :: without purpose : _____

   Ⓐ intently   Ⓑ collectively   Ⓒ drastically   ⬤ aimlessly

8. quick : slow :: kind : _____

   Ⓐ unyielding   Ⓑ obstinate   ⬤ merciless   Ⓓ elegant

9. bleak : bare :: rustic : _____

   Ⓐ full   Ⓑ dignified   Ⓒ dirty   ⬤ simple

10. heavily decorated : ornate :: extravagant : _____

    Ⓐ brittle   ⬤ lavish   Ⓒ brisk   Ⓓ hopeful

11. splurge : extravagant :: rampage : _____

    Ⓐ generous   Ⓑ satisfying   Ⓒ dirty   ⬤ destructive

12. indistinct : obvious :: average : _____

    Ⓐ gullible   ⬤ exceptional   Ⓒ impudent   Ⓓ intentional

Lesson 23Answer Key 0272867

1. hide : conceal :: disappear : _____

   Ⓐ bandit　　Ⓑ suspect　　Ⓒ hide　　● **vanish**

2. complaint : _____ :: disability : handicap
   ● **grievance**　　Ⓑ principle　　Ⓒ altercation　　Ⓓ archive

3. unsure : absolute :: mild : _____

   Ⓐ scarce　　● **extreme**　　Ⓒ easy　　Ⓓ negative

4. a penalty given to someone for doing wrong : punishment :: getting back at someone who has done something to hurt you : _____

   Ⓐ grievance　　Ⓑ penance　　Ⓒ munitions　　● **revenge**

5. without giving up : relentlessly :: on purpose : _____
   Ⓐ vigorously　　● **deliberately**　　Ⓒ mournfully　　Ⓓ grudgingly

6. a marketable good : commodity :: an illness : _____

   Ⓐ chattel　　● **malady**　　Ⓒ branch　　Ⓓ adder

7. _____ : practical :: excessive : extravagant

   ● **sensible**　　Ⓑ bold　　Ⓒ showy　　Ⓓ urgent

8. extravagant : luxurious :: preposterous : _____

   ● **absurd**　　Ⓑ hidden　　Ⓒ scared　　Ⓓ unquestionable

9. careful : cautious :: purposeful : _____
   Ⓐ apprehensive　　● **deliberate**　　Ⓒ luxurious　　Ⓓ oppressive

10. consign : entrust :: perambulate : _____

    Ⓐ forgive　　Ⓑ hide　　● **walk**　　Ⓓ write

11. hidden : concealed :: pulled out : _____

    ● **plucked**　　Ⓑ fainted　　Ⓒ herded　　Ⓓ pushed

12. real : authentic :: intentional : _____
    Ⓐ plausible　　Ⓑ vigorous　　● **deliberate**　　Ⓓ apprehensive

Lesson 24
Answer Key 0272867

1. abhor : _____ :: stun : shock

   (A) kiss　　　(B) scream　　　- hate　　　(D) sharing

2. a penalty given to someone for doing wrong : punishment :: getting back at someone who has done something to hurt you : _____

   ● revenge　　　(B) munitions　　　(C) grievance　　　(D) penance

3. quick : slow :: kind : _____

   ● merciless　　　(B) obstinate　　　(C) elegant　　　(D) unyielding

4. quick and light : nimble :: thick : _____

   (A) foul　　　(B) drastic　　　● dense　　　(D) crass

5. absurd : preposterous :: disbelieving : _____

   (A) relentless　　　● incredulous　　　(C) logical　　　(D) impudent

6. a marketable good : commodity :: an illness : _____

   (A) adder　　　(B) chattel　　　(C) branch　　　● malady

7. abundant : _____ :: drastic : extreme

   (A) loud　　　(B) uninhabited　　　● plentiful　　　. truthful

8. splurge : extravagant :: rampage : _____

   (A) satisfying　　　● destructive　　　(C) dirty　　　(D) generous

9. fetter : bind :: _____ : pretend

   (A) picket　　　(B) impart　　　● feign　　　(D) abate

10. _____ : practical :: excessive : extravagant

    (A) urgent　　　● sensible　　　(C) bold　　　(D) showy

11. _____ : ominous :: purposeful : deliberate

    ● threatening　　　(B) sad　　　(C) truthful　　　(D) serene

12. _____ : persuade :: pretend : imagine

    (A) forgive　　　(B) hide　　　(C) leave　　　● convince

Lesson 25
Answer Key 0200817

1. disinterest : boredom :: contentment : _____

   Ⓐ anger   Ⓑ relief   Ⓒ resentment   ● happiness

2. _____ : against the law :: illiterate : cannot read

   . secretive   Ⓑ charitable   ● illegal   . lawful

3. boisterous : _____ :: sympathetic : understanding

   Ⓐ silent   Ⓑ tight   . serious   ● loud

4. tiredness : _____ :: daydreaming : reverie

   Ⓐ precaution   . solace   ● fatigue   Ⓓ monotony

5. diligent : hardworking :: clever : _____

   Ⓐ lever   Ⓑ nice   Ⓒ brainless   ● smart

6. abrupt : sudden :: broad : _____

   Ⓐ narrow   ● wide   Ⓒ odd   Ⓓ slow

7. intense emotion : fervor :: boredom : _____

   ● tedium   Ⓑ chivalry   Ⓒ scourge   Ⓓ prestige

8. ending : interminable :: barren : _____

   ● fertile   Ⓑ permitted   Ⓒ nimble   Ⓓ discriminate

9. achievement : accomplishment :: praise : _____

   Ⓐ opponent   ● accolades   Ⓒ criticism   . reverence

10. conciliating : soothing :: imperious : _____

    ● bossy   Ⓑ irritating   Ⓒ helpful   Ⓓ frightening

11. happy : sad :: excited : _____

    ● disappointed   Ⓑ shocked   Ⓒ disgusted   Ⓓ confused

12. frantic : frenzied :: elated : _____

    Ⓐ relaxed   ● overjoyed   Ⓒ surprised   Ⓓ disgusted

Lesson 26
Answer Key 0200817

1. hysteria : panic :: epidemic : _____

   Ⓐ depredation   Ⓑ stampede   Ⓒ rogue   ● plague

2. purchased : bought :: attempted : _____

   ● tried   Ⓑ used   sold   Ⓓ proven

3. _____ : tired :: meek : shy

   Ⓐ daunted   Ⓑ scanty   ● weary   Ⓓ thwarted

4. obstreperous : unruly :: adroit : _____

   ● skillful   Ⓑ curious   Ⓒ generous   Ⓓ humane

5. animosity : hostility :: trepidation : _____
   ● fear   Ⓑ confidence   Ⓒ hope   Ⓓ bravery

6. disappear : vanish :: fear : _____
   evaporate   Ⓑ bravery   ● terrify   Ⓓ emerge

7. canny : careful :: frank : _____

   Ⓐ trusting   ● honest   Ⓒ bold   Ⓓ generous

8. tiredness : _____ :: daydreaming : reverie
   Ⓐ monotony   Ⓑ solace   Ⓒ precaution   ● fatigue

9. _____ : doubtful :: demure : modest

   Ⓐ gruff   Ⓑ languid   ● dubious   Ⓓ malevolent

10. happy : sad :: excited : _____
    Ⓐ disgusted   Ⓑ confused   Ⓒ shocked   ● disappointed

11. soothe : calm :: elongate : _____

    Ⓐ aggravate   shorten   ● lengthen   Ⓓ honor

12. enthusiastic : ardent :: skillful : _____

    Ⓐ barbarous   ● dexterous   Ⓒ solitary   Ⓓ fervid

<table>
<tr><td colspan="4">**Lesson 27**
Answer Key 0200817</td></tr>
</table>

1. patriotism : pride :: terrorism : _____

   (A) hope   . retaliation   ● **fear**   (D) indifference

2. calm : panicky :: relaxed : _____

   - **tense**   (B) elegant   (C) swift   (D) insufficient

3. ordinary : special :: humble : _____

   (A) shallow   ● **vain**   . keen   (D) distressed

4. search : look for :: _____ : find

   ● **discover**   (B) extinct   (C) mystery   (D) dinosaurs

5. hysteria : panic :: epidemic : _____

   (A) rogue   (B) stampede   ● **plague**   (D) depredation

6. an expression of approval or honor : praise :: an admission of wrongdoings : _____

   (A) commitment   (B) ecology   ● **confession**   (D) impression

7. tumultuous : disorderly :: _____ : horrible

   (A) brave   (B) frightening   (C) humbling   ● **gruesome**

8. chintzy : stingy :: skeptical : _____

   (A) stubborn   - **doubtful**   (C) helpful   (D) strong

9. perfunctory : unconcerned :: wayward : _____

   ● **unruly**   . meddling   (C) reluctant   (D) clumsy

10. find : discover :: uncover : _____

    (A) endure   (B) retract   ● **excavate**   (D) fossil

11. happy : sad :: calm : _____

    (A) sleepy   (B) funny   . still   ● **panic**

12. diminutive : gigantic :: defiant : _____

    (A) feeble   ● **obedient**   (C) tremulous   (D) willful

Lesson 28
Answer Key 0289106

1. deceive : mislead :: decipher : _____

   (A) announce   (B) analyze   ● solve   (D) confuse

2. the variation of a language in a particular region : dialect :: a group of stars forming a shape in the sky : _____
   (A) pinnacle   (B) plume   ● constellation   (D) corridor

3. not enough rain : drought :: too much rain : _____

   ● flood   (B) infestation   (C) famine   (D) fertile

4. drastic : moderate :: ancient : _____

   ● juvenile   (B) artifact   history   (D) extreme

5. rude : insolent :: capable : _____
   (A) dejected   (B) hardy   ● competent   (D) epic

6. to set on fire : ignite :: to empty : _____

   (A) conform   (B) invigorate   (C) gorge   ● vacate

7. joyful : happy :: celebrate : _____

   (A) mourn   ● honor   (C) sad   (D) contemplate

8. leave : depart :: settle : _____
   (A) travel   ● colonize   (C) celebrate   (D) land

9. perplexed : confused :: jocund : _____

   (A) greedy   angry   (C) old   ● cheerful

10. lament : mourn :: cajole : _____
    (A) tease   (B) celebrate   ● persuade   (D) teach

11. blaming someone else for your mistake : lying :: copying someone else's homework : _____

    (A) morals   (B) impolite   (C) greedy   ● cheating

12. plume : pen :: _____ : paper
    (A) pencil   ● parchment   (C) brocade   (D) diagram

Lesson 29
Answer Key 0289106

1. build : construct :: sell : _____

   Ⓐ price   Ⓑ design   ⬤ **market**   Ⓓ distribute

2. light : heavy :: weak : _____
   Ⓐ change   Ⓑ endanger   − **strong**   Ⓓ dull

3. plume : feather :: talon : _____

   Ⓐ eye   Ⓑ wing   Ⓒ beak   − **claw**

4. leave : depart :: settle : _____
   Ⓐ travel   ⬤ **colonize**   Ⓒ celebrate   Ⓓ land

5. lament : mourn :: cajole : _____

   Ⓐ tease   Ⓑ celebrate   Ⓒ teach   ⬤ **persuade**

6. to estimate incorrectly : miscalculate :: to adjust to new conditions : _____

   ⬤ **adapt**   Ⓑ justify   Ⓒ navigate   Ⓓ avenge

7. _____ : generous :: cold-hearted : empathetic
   Ⓐ pleased   Ⓑ piteous   ⬤ **greedy**   Ⓓ astonishing

8. amplify : intensify :: differentiate : _____

   Ⓐ encourage   . adapt   ⬤ **distinguish**   Ⓓ lead

9. replenish : _____ :: squelch : crush
   Ⓐ discuss   ⬤ **refill**   Ⓒ regret   Ⓓ lurk

10. guess : speculate :: look forward to : _____

    Ⓐ exhilarate   Ⓑ apprehend   ⬤ **anticipate**   Ⓓ review

11. something that happened previously : preceding :: something that will happen soon : _____

    ⬤ **impending**   Ⓑ coinciding   Ⓒ postponed   Ⓓ subsiding

12. torment : disturb :: replenish : _____

    Ⓐ discuss   Ⓑ regret   ⬤ **refill**   Ⓓ lurk

> **Lesson 30**
> **Answer Key 0289106**

1. sorrowful : sad :: complicated : _____
   - Ⓐ intensive
   - Ⓑ complete
   - Ⓒ blunt
   - ● **complex**

2. erratic : unpredictable :: nonchalant : _____
   - Ⓐ rippled
   - ● **casual**
   - Ⓒ indistinct
   - Ⓓ dense

3. build : construct :: sell : _____
   - ● **market**
   - Ⓑ distribute
   - Ⓒ price
   - Ⓓ design

4. unemotional : impassive :: hopeful : _____
   - Ⓐ presumptuous
   - Ⓑ sarcastic
   - ● **optimistic**
   - Ⓓ hospitable

5. parasol : umbrella :: confection : _____
   - Ⓐ announcement
   - Ⓑ sword
   - Ⓒ competition
   - ● **candy**

6. magazine : issue :: television program : _____
   - Ⓐ record
   - ● **episode**
   - Ⓒ movie
   - Ⓓ page

7. majestic : regal :: complex : _____
   - ● **intricate**
   - Ⓑ delicate
   - Ⓒ derivative
   - Ⓓ simple

8. poor soil where nothing can grow : barren :: rich soil that is good for farming : _____
   - Ⓐ nimble
   - Ⓑ discriminate
   - Ⓒ sparse
   - ● **fertile**

9. drastic : moderate :: ancient : _____
   - Ⓐ extreme
   - ● **juvenile**
   - Ⓒ history
   - Ⓓ artifact

10. articulate : eloquent :: intricate : _____
    - ● **complex**
    - Ⓑ smooth
    - Ⓒ delicate
    - Ⓓ simple

11. sumac : plant :: calico : _____
    - ● **fabric**
    - Ⓑ rafters
    - Ⓒ food
    - Ⓓ ravine

12. fierce : timid :: greedy : _____
    - Ⓐ hopeful
    - Ⓑ jealous
    - _ charitable
    - Ⓓ sympathetic

Lesson 31
Answer Key 0944077

1. gleeful : _____ :: dismayed : disappointed

   . shy   **B** furious   ⬤ **happy**   **D** confused

2. naive : gullible :: uppity : _____

   A shrewd   **B** rational   **C** disoriented   ⬤ **presumptuous**

3. negative : electrons :: positive : _____

   A cells   ⬤ **protons**   **C** atoms   **D** neutrons

4. to calm : placate :: to spread out : _____

   A provoke   **B** careen   ⬤ **disperse**   **D** subside

5. quick : slow :: kind : _____

   A obstinate   **B** unyielding   ⬤ **merciless**   **D** elegant

6. peak : mountain :: _____ : house

   ⬤ **roof**   **B** fire   **C** floor   **D** door

7. debatable : controversial :: unopposed : _____

   A inclusive   **B** sarcastic   **C** metropolitan   ⬤ **unanimous**

8. disturb : perturb :: fascinate : _____

   A subside   ⬤ **intrigue**   **C** decipher   **D** muster

9. mooring : securing :: meddling : _____

   A sheltering   **B** endangering   **C** dividing   ⬤ **interfering**

10. an illusion : hallucination :: a wide view : _____

   ⬤ **panorama**   **B** horizon   **C** multimedia   **D** peak

11. mournful : _____ :: obstinate : stubborn

   A coached   **B** haunted   ⬤ **sorrowful**   **D** honorable

12. a guess : speculation :: a goal : _____

   A admonition   **B** devotion   . fate   ⬤ **aspiration**

Lesson 32
Answer Key 0944077

1. curious : interested in how things work :: persevere : _____

    ● does not give up   Ⓑ refuses to change   Ⓒ scatterbrained   Ⓓ smart

2. revive : renew :: thrive : _____
    Ⓐ control   Ⓑ replenish   Ⓒ accept   ● prosper

3. to move clumsily : lumber :: to attack : _____

    Ⓐ subside   Ⓑ clamor   ● assail   Ⓓ resent

4. unsure : absolute :: mild : _____
    Ⓐ negative   Ⓑ cold   Ⓒ easy   ● extreme

5. a small stream : creek :: a range of hills or mountains : _____

    Ⓐ bank   ● ridge   Ⓒ breech   Ⓓ peak

6. sentimental : emotional :: optimistic : _____

    ● hopeful   Ⓑ humorous   Ⓒ negative   Ⓓ ridiculous

7. guess : speculate :: look forward to : _____
    Ⓐ cremate   Ⓑ exhilarate   Ⓒ distribute   ● anticipate

8. excited by frustration or nervousness : frantic :: careful : _____

    Ⓐ alert   ● cautious   Ⓒ far away   Ⓓ unknown

9. worsen : improve :: disappoint : _____
    ● impress   Ⓑ petition   Ⓒ yearn   Ⓓ relinquish

10. careful : cautious :: purposeful : _____

    Ⓐ oppressive   ● deliberate   Ⓒ luxurious   Ⓓ apprehensive

11. recognize : identify :: subside : _____

    Ⓐ lengthen   Ⓑ disappear   ● diminish   Ⓓ hide

12. to calm : placate :: to spread out : _____
    ● disperse   Ⓑ provoke   Ⓒ careen   Ⓓ subside

Lesson 33
Answer Key 0944077

1. diminish : subside :: twist together : _____

   Ⓐ imbue   Ⓑ conquer   ⬤ entwine   Ⓓ relent

2. peer : look :: spurn : _____
   ⬤ reject   Ⓑ hide   Ⓒ warn   Ⓓ purchase

3. falter : advance :: abandon : _____

   Ⓐ hope   Ⓑ forward   Ⓒ lose   ⬤ rescue

4. to fear greatly : _____ :: to look forward to : anticipate

   ⬤ dread   Ⓑ evaporate   Ⓒ perceive   Ⓓ apprehend

5. funny : hilarious :: pitiful : _____
   Ⓐ gullible   Ⓑ generic   ⬤ pathetic   Ⓓ disproportionate

6. peak : mountain :: _____ : house
   Ⓐ floor   Ⓑ fire   ⬤ roof   Ⓓ door

7. to strive toward a goal : aspire :: to work together : _____

   Ⓐ transfix   Ⓑ resume   Ⓒ embark   ⬤ collaborate

8. Relax : unwind :: Labor : _____

   Ⓐ retire   ⬤ work   Ⓒ job   Ⓓ employ

9. stubborn : obstinate :: unashamed : _____
   Ⓐ deprived   Ⓑ inoculated   Ⓒ antebellum   ⬤ unabashed

10. genuine : phony :: fragile : _____

   Ⓐ unbearable   Ⓑ amphibious   Ⓒ inside   ⬤ indestructible

11. flourish : wave :: perspire : _____

   Ⓐ reach   ⬤ sweat   Ⓒ cut   Ⓓ speak

12. to move clumsily : lumber :: to attack : _____

   Ⓐ subside   Ⓑ clamor   ⬤ assail   Ⓓ resent

Made in the USA
Monee, IL
02 December 2021

83679584R00083